REIKI AND CHRISTIAN HEALING

By The Rev. Alice Mindrum

Edited by Nancy A. Hedberg

Front cover design by Richard Hagedus
Hagedus Graphic Design

ISBN13 978-1-59518-061-2
ISBN 1-59518-061-3

LEADERRESOURCES

P.O. Box 302
Leeds, MA 01053
Phone: 800-941-2218
staff@LeaderResources.org

www.LeaderResources.org

TABLE OF CONTENTS

FOREWARD

by The Rt. Rev. Ian T. Douglas, Bishop of Connecticut

There is lots of talk in the Church today about mission. Understandings of mission are moving beyond 19th and early 20th century perspectives of mission as being well-meaning Christians from the industrialized West seeking to convert peoples in Asia, Africa, and Latin America. The meaning of mission is even growing beyond a previously church-centered focus on sharing our abundance with those who seem to have less. No, today mission is less about activities in some far-flung place, or the work of the Church. Rather mission today is trending towards a focus on God and God's action—what God is up to in the world.

Contemporary perspectives on mission start with the mission of God, the *missio Dei*. Here the mission of God is to bring about a right-ordered creation where brokenness, alienation, division, and suffering give way to restoration, reconciliation, wholeness, and health. Paraphrasing *The Book of Common Prayer* of The Episcopal Church, the mission of God is "to restore all people to unity with God and each other in Christ." (BCP p. 855) Restored unity with God and each other is what God wants for all people and all creation. Restored unity with God and each other is fundamentally about healing. God's mission is all about healing.

Even a cursory read of Christian scripture reveals that healing is central to what God is up to in Jesus Christ. The Gospels, in particular, reflect the centrality of healing to Jesus' life and ministry. Dozens and dozens of stories tell of how Jesus effected healing and wholeness for those who were sick, those who were marginalized, and those who were alienated from God, from themselves, from society, and from creation. Jesus, as the Messiah, was an agent of God's healing Spirit in the world. Jesus, as God incarnate, shared in God's mission to restore all people to unity with God and each other. God's mission in Jesus was and is to effect restoration, reconciliation, wholeness, and healing among all people and with all creation.

The healing vocation of Jesus was not limited to him as the Messiah, the Son of God. The apostles and disciples were equally commissioned, co-missioned in God's healing mission in the world.

In the Gospels and Acts of the Apostles we hear of how the followers of Jesus were agents of healing, agents of the in-breaking of the reign of God where all is made well in a new restored, and reconciled creation. When Jesus sent out the seventy, he commissioned them to heal the sick and proclaim that the kingdom of God has come near. Healing of individuals and creation is a marker of the reality of God's kingdom, God's reign. All followers of Jesus are called to be agents of this healing mission of God in Jesus by the power of the Holy Spirit.

From this perspective of the mission of God, Alice Mindrum's brief and accessible book *Reiki and Christian Healing* has a significant contribution to make. Alice's invitation to Christians and others to try on the possibility that in Reiki, the "divine spirit" is effecting healing is a welcome addition to discussions of what God is up to in the world. Through story telling, hers and others', Alice breaks down prejudices about what Reiki is. Drawing on Christian scripture, she adeptly helps the reader to see how Reiki is consistent with the healing ministry of Jesus and his followers.

What comes through in these pages is a portrait of a devout and generous Christian leader who has been touched by the divine spirit. Mindrum's exploration of the roots and realities of Reiki is at one and the same time both comprehensive and eminently readable. She invites those of us who are followers of Jesus to expand our understanding, and even practice, of God's healing mission in our lives, the lives of others, and in the world. Reading *Reiki and Christian Healing* thus offers new possibilities and perspectives to serve God's mission of healing and wholeness. Encountering the divine spirit in new ways brings us deeper into the call to restore all people to unity with God and each other in Christ.

INTRODUCTION

What is Reiki? And what, if anything, has it got to do with Christian healing?

As an Episcopal priest who is also a Reiki master teacher, I am often asked these sorts of questions by fellow Christians. Typically, those doing the asking fall into one of the following groups.

The first group consists of Christians who have never heard of Reiki until I mention it. Some are interested and curious when I describe the theory and practice of Reiki healing, while others look puzzled or politely skeptical about the whole concept. If you are reading this book because you know little or nothing about Reiki but you would like to find out more, I hope that within these pages you will find informative answers to your questions.

The second group is made up of those who have received Reiki healing themselves, usually in a health care or spa environment. Those who have experienced Reiki in a hospital or other medical setting—and these numbers are expanding as the good news of Reiki spreads—are usually grateful for the role Reiki played in their healing, and clear in their understanding of its value. People who experienced Reiki in a spa environment are strong proponents of Reiki as well, but less focused on its healing properties and more familiar with the deep relaxation which it offers. They may not realize that such relaxation allows the body to do what God created it to do: to heal. If you have received Reiki and would like to know more about its history and practice—particularly in light of the Christian healing mission—I hope this book will help you accomplish that.

The third group of questioners consists of theologically conservative Christians. These folks are clearly skeptical when the topic of Reiki comes up, although they don't often speak directly to me about it. Usually their questions and/or criticisms regarding Reiki are brought to me by my students.

Regrettably, people who cast aspersions on Reiki often have little knowledge or firsthand experience of it. Frequently they are repeating the opinions of others whose pronouncements they accept without question. And ironically, the group invested with the authority to judge Reiki often has little accurate information itself.

Reiki is sometimes dismissed out of hand by people suspicious of a healing technique not overtly Christian in origin. These folks sincerely maintain that Reiki and Jesus don't mix. If you fall into this category, please keep reading. I hope by the end of this book your perspective will have changed—and even if you are not convinced, at least you will be better informed!

Finally—and happily—there is a growing number of Christians who feel drawn to learn about Reiki and who have a vision of its value in the Christian healing mission. But despite their conviction that Reiki is a gift from God, they may find themselves tongue-tied and confused when asked to explain why. And when they hear negative judgments of Reiki from other more conservative Christians, they may feel uncertain and secretly wonder if they are mistaken in thinking that Reiki is an acceptable Christian healing technique.

If you recognize yourself in the paragraph above, this book is written with you particularly in mind. I hope that it will provide you with thoughtful and informed responses to questions which may come your way, and that it will help put to rest any concerns you may have about practicing Reiki. Ideally, all Christian Reiki practitioners would be able to discuss their personal theology of healing, and the way in which Reiki fits into it.

In the chapters which follow you will find the story of Reiki and my own introduction to it. You will be learn how Reiki "works," as well as the ways in which Reiki can be taught, learned and practiced, particularly in the Christian context. We will explore Reiki through the lens of Christian scripture and the history of our healing tradition. Chapter Seven examines ways in which Reiki can be part of a faithful Christian life and Chapter Eight contains interviews with Reiki practitioners from five of the world's largest religions: Buddhism, Christianity, Hinduism, Islam and Judaism. You may be startled by the common themes and responses they share. Finally, Chapter Nine contains stories of Reiki healing from the practitioner's viewpoint, and also from the perspective of Christians who have received Reiki. Personal stories are an inspirational way to explore Reiki.

Whoever you are and wherever you find yourself regarding Reiki and Christian healing, I offer this work to you with a prayer that God will bless you through it, and that you will be guided into a deeper understanding of your own healing ministry. If you are Christian, I hope that this book will illuminate your understanding of Reiki and God's great healing mission. If you are not Christian, whatever spiritual tradition you follow can be equally enriched by the practice of Reiki.

The Rev. Alice Mindrum
Southport CT, December 2011

This book is dedicated to
all my teachers

CHAPTER ONE

DISCOVERING REIKI

My Story

I first heard of Reiki (pronounced "RAY-kee") in the early '90's when I read a newspaper article about a well-known opera singer who had twisted his ankle just prior to a performance. Great consternation ensued. Then a young woman from the orchestra stepped forward and offered to give him Reiki. The desperate singer agreed, and the young woman laid her hands on the injured area for several moments. Fairly quickly the pain lessened and the singer could walk without a limp, at least for the duration of the performance.

I had always been interested in healing, and wished that I could help someone as effectively as the newspaper had described. But I also believed that there was no training that could impart the ability to heal; it was something you either had, or you didn't. I didn't.

About this same time I began attending Yale Divinity School. It was a time of great change in my life; my husband traveled regularly, and with our three sons growing up I had much more flexibility in my schedule than previously. The world beyond family and friends beckoned, offering exciting opportunities for work and service. But then my life took an unexpected turn, and my interest in healing became personal.

Two months after graduation I was diagnosed with early stage Hodgkin's Lymphoma. Soon I was commuting to New Haven again, not to classes but to chemotherapy at the Yale-New Haven Hospital. It was a supremely difficult time, but our family was blessed by the generous support of relatives and friends.

As often happens, in terms of spiritual growth this hard time was also a fruitful time. I learned lessons then that strongly impacted my belief system, and which still affect the way I live. My theological perspective broadened, and my personal experience with illness increased my desire to help alleviate suffering in the world.

Our family was active in a local Episcopal church and so we were blessed with access to extensive prayer support. I shamelessly requested prayers from anyone who asked how they could help, and I know those prayers sustained my family and me during that tough time.

My journey to wellness was grounded in traditional Western healing methods and bolstered with what were then called alternative therapies. While my experienced and wonderful doctor ordered medical treatments, my techno-savvy husband Tom delved into the new online medical websites—and I explored complementary healing techniques. I read up on nutrition and environmental health issues and added yoga, massage and chiropractic sessions to my self care regime. Healing services, prayer groups, classes, and workshops focusing on physical, emotional, and/or spiritual health were effective and endlessly fascinating. Friends and colleagues alerted me to lectures or books they thought I would find helpful, and that was why the Rev. Ben Brockman mentioned the work of Dr. Caroline Myss to me.

Learning from Dr. Caroline Myss

Dr. Myss is a popular contemporary teacher of spirituality and healing, and she wields enormous and positive influence in the field of energetic healing. Her particular focus is on the connection between physical dis-ease and spiritual/emotional matters, so her materials fit quite naturally into the areas I was already exploring. I listened to her tapes and read her books with great interest but also with caution, because—as the colleague who had mentioned her warned me—in addition to their wisdom there was also material foreign to me as an orthodox Christian. Indeed, the discussion of some points in Dr. Myss's teaching seemed to lack a full understanding of contemporary Christian theology.

Even so, I appreciated Dr. Myss's frequent scriptural references, her Christian roots, and her extensive knowledge of other religions. She has a dry sense of humor and great pragmatism, combined with a gift for fresh insights. Her theories about healing, though sometimes expressed in unfamiliar terms, resonated with my own experience and beliefs. In the end I took the advice of a wise nun: treasure what is helpful, and ignore what is not. (What she actually said was, "Take the meat and leave the bones!") This attitude has served me well in my exploration of spirituality and healing.

Not long after I was deemed officially cured of cancer, I began the process of seeking ordination in the Episcopal Church. I was so grateful for all the years I had worked in the Church as a lay person, and for all the ways in which the Church—and her ministers—had helped me to know and delight in God's presence in my life. I loved the Church's intentional call to diversity—both human and ideological—and its rich sacramental life. I felt blessed that I had been led to this wonderful vocation, in which I could work and serve God in the company of others on a conscious spiritual path.

Early Days of My Ministry

My journey to the priesthood brought Reiki to my attention once again. During the required hospital chaplaincy training, I met a Protestant minister who was also a Reiki practitioner. She lectured on the value of Reiki in hospital, nursing home, and hospice settings, and she gave each class member a few moments of Reiki. When she declared that Reiki could be learned by anyone who desired to do so—a sentiment far from my Christian understanding of the matter—I was inspired to decide that someday in the not-too-distant future I would find a way to study Reiki.

My first post-ordination position was in a small parish. Having received a good-sized grant to develop a healing ministry, the parish started a health center ministry they named "Open Doors." Among the activities offered through the Center were affordable private healing sessions, group classes and workshops teaching meditation, yoga, healing through art and music, and healing touch methods, including Reiki. The Reiki demonstration reaffirmed my interest in seeking training, and shortly afterward I began studying Reiki with Gigi Benanti, whose Reiki practice was (and is) located not far from the church.

Over the next two years I studied Reiki Levels One, Two, and Three (Master level). Every morning and evening I practiced Reiki on myself; it felt wonderfully relaxing. Several months after I began to do this, it dawned on me that I had gone through the winter without a sinus infection, which was unheard of for me. In addition, I started to notice that my emotions were less volatile—much more harmonized and peaceful. And the following summer I made the happy discovery that Reiki could short circuit my annual dose of poison ivy. Instead of needing steroids to rid myself of the dreaded rash—I am an enthusiastic gardener—I found that using Reiki over two or three days would prevent it from getting a good start. Although there is poison ivy stubbornly growing along one edge of our property, over the past decade I have used steroids only once to get rid of the resultant rash. (That was the time I apparently knelt on the horrible weed, and since I had to wear a dress to a wedding soon after I didn't have time to wait for the Reiki to eradicate the blisters. I took the Prednisone and was grateful for it!)

Once I was convinced that Reiki benefited my own health I was more comfortable offering it to parishioners during pastoral calls. I explained to the recipients that Reiki simply means "spiritual energy" or "divine energy" in Japanese. In this way they came to understand that Reiki healing is based on the use of God's creative and healing energy. While the recipient(s) and I sat together—often just chatting after an initial few moments of prayer—I would lay my hands on his or her hands and shoulders and head and feet (not all at once!) and we would continue our prayer through Reiki—which is really just a hands-on, focused, nonverbal form of prayer. Often I would ask them to place their own hands on or near the affected area at the same time. Since Reiki doesn't require disrobing, lotions or any special equipment, it was simple to use at any time and any place.

Parishioners began giving me positive feedback after these brief and relaxed sessions, happily reporting improved pain levels, alleviated anxiety, increased feelings of peace, and deeper, more restful sleep. These affirming responses were important because even I was having trouble believing how effective Reiki was. Despite my teacher's assurances that anyone who was dedicated

14

could learn to channel Reiki, I had remained secretly doubtful that I would be able to do so.

During those months I learned a crucial—and encouraging—lesson: that, regardless of what the practitioner is feeling, God's energy (the Reiki) will flow. We can put aside our egos and let the work of the Holy Spirit take center stage since the healing does not come from us, but from God. All we need to do is remain faithful and focused, and trust that the Spirit knows what needs to happen next.

Reiki remains an important part of my life. I often use it in pastoral care, sometimes with little apparent effect and at other times with striking results—as happened recently when one of my colleagues asked for a Reiki session to try and ease his agonizing 21-day-old case of shingles. He called me, exultant, the day following our session, to report that his pain was gone. It never returned, apart from an occasional brief and mild twinge as the healing continued. He was so grateful he declared he was going to spread the word about Reiki to everybody he knew.

The various churches where I've worked have all explored different ways to integrate Reiki into their parish healing ministries. This requires patience and perseverance, and some approaches have worked better than others. Currently I am aware of Reiki practitioners who offer free home or health care visits (working in pairs) at the recommendation of the rector; parishioners who are Reiki volunteers in hospitals; healing services which integrate Reiki healing into the liturgy; groups of church members who are also Reiki practitioners and who gather to share Reiki among themselves as well as discuss their experiences (carefully protecting the confidentiality of those with whom they work). The Reiki method of healing can be an effective part of the Christian healing mission, and no doubt the future will offer many more ways for us to use it fruitfully.

I love teaching Reiki and I do so regularly; the good news of Reiki always seems to get around. Graduates of my classes gather regularly to share Reiki and our Reiki stories with one another, and to offer prayers and send Reiki to those in need of it. Opportunities to enrich life through Reiki abound, and it's good to know that we can make a positive difference in our own and other people's lives.

For anyone wishing to help ease the pain and suffering in the world, Reiki is a remarkable healing method and integrates easily—even inevitably—into the Christian healing mission, since it utilizes the energy (Spirit) of God. Sometimes it just seems too good to be true, and I find myself fumbling for words to try and explain it adequately. At such times I am reminded of the Roman Catholic priest who was asked why he prayed the Rosary. "Because it works." he said.

I find his answer simple and direct. I practice Reiki because it works.

THE STORY OF REIKI

CHAPTER TWO

In The Beginning

The founder of Usui Reiki was Dr. Mikao Usui, a Japanese gentleman born August 15, 1864 in the village of Yago, Japan; he died on March 9, 1926. Mikao Usui was not a medical doctor; the term "Dr." is commonly used as a respectful honorific. Since Dr. Usui passed on fewer than one hundred years ago, one might expect that obtaining information on his life and the beginnings of Reiki would be easily done, but this has not been the case. A number of obstacles have interfered with the story of Reiki becoming known in the West.

One stumbling block to finding information on Reiki's origins is that the Japanese have traditionally been a private people. When this quality is combined with the polarizing effects of World War II, the breakdown in communication between East and West regarding Reiki seems not only understandable, but inevitable. Incredibly, for a long time we in the West were so disconnected from the Japanese school of Usui Reiki that we mistakenly believed Reiki no longer survived in Japan.

A second obstacle to learning the history of Reiki has been the reluctance of Mikao Usui's relatives to speak of him or his involvement with Reiki. In 1993 Chetna Kobayashi, a Reiki Master then married to Master and author Frank Arjava Petter, was able to speak with the wife of Dr. Usui's grandson. During their conversation, the granddaughter-in-law stressed that the family is very unwilling to talk about Dr. Usui with outsiders, and that his daughter (now deceased) had actually left "a clause in her will stating that his name should never be mentioned in her house."[1]

Following the interview, Kobayashi and Petter received a letter from the granddaughter-in-law reiterating that she was not allowed to talk about the matter, and requesting that they not contact her again. They respected her wishes, but happily discovered other sources through which to pursue their inquiries.[2]

We can only speculate as to why such aversion to Dr. Usui's memory exists among his descendants. Certainly history shows that visionaries often find themselves unwelcome among their friends and family. Jesus' famous quote seems apt: "Prophets are not without honor, except in their hometown, and among their own kin, and in their own house." (Mark 6:4)[3]

The silence of Dr. Usui's family helped misinformation about him to proliferate unchallenged. One mistaken yet commonly held belief was that Mikao Usui was a Christian, a graduate of the University of Chicago who ran a Christian seminary in Japan. Over the past decade or so as new information has come to light, these and other incorrect assumptions have been debunked.

We now know that Dr. Usui was a Buddhist and a student of many subjects, including philosophy and various religions. The Reiki healing system, however, is no more Buddhist than it is Christian, for Reiki is not a religion but rather a method of healing which utilizes divine energy. This universal energy—known in Christianity as the Holy Spirit, the life energy flowing from God and Christ—is available to all people, not simply to members of one religion. Thus, while Reiki is compatible with all religions, it is limited to none, for Reiki is a spiritual rather than a religious healing method.

Perhaps Mikao Usui's Buddhist roots were ignored because it was feared that the West would reject any healing modality not Christian in origin. Sadly, the fact that some contemporary Christians do indeed reject Reiki as "anti-Christian" confirms the validity of this concern.

Time passed, and by the late 20th century resentments left from World War II were fading, Westerners were more open to Eastern ideas, and vice versa. Through the efforts of Western Reiki masters such as Frank Arjava Petter and William Lee Rand, as well as with the help of Japanese Reiki master Mr. Hiroshi Doi—a member of the Usui Reiki Ryoho Gakkai—details about the origins of Reiki have become better known outside Japan.[4] As new information emerges, the Western understanding of Reiki's history and its current practice in Japan has been revised and updated.

Reiki and Dr. Usui

Dr. Usui is buried in the cemetery at the Pure Land Buddhist Saihoji temple in Tokyo. A memorial stone was placed there one year after his passing by a number of his students who were members of the Usui Reiki Ryoho Gakkai. The earliest information we have comes from this memorial stone.

Frank Arjava Petter and Chetna Kobayashi visited Dr. Usui's gravesite and memorial stone in the Toyotama District of Tokyo. The stone was inscribed in old Japanese by Juzaburo Ushida and Masayuki Okada, and the contemporary Japanese translation which follows was made by Masano Kobayashi, Chetna Kobayashi's mother.

The whole text is reprinted below with the kind permission of author Frank Arjava Petter and Lotus Light Publications.[5]

Photo courtesy of William Rand (www.reiki.org)

Dr. Usui's Memorial Inscription

Someone who studies hard and works assiduously to improve body and mind for the sake of becoming a better person is called "a man of great spirit." People who use that great spirit for a social purpose, that is, to teach the right way to many people and do collective good, are called "teachers." Dr. Usui was one such teacher. He taught the Reiki of the universe. Countless people came to him and asked him to teach them the great way of Reiki and to heal them.

Dr. Usui was born in the first year of the Keio period, called Keio gunnen, on August 15th (1864)....From what is known, he was a talented and hard-working student. As an adult he traveled to several Western countries and China to study, worked arduously, but did at (some) point run into some bad luck. However he didn't give up and trained himself arduously.

One day he went to Mount Kurama on a 21-day retreat to fast and meditate. At the end of this period he suddenly felt the great Reiki energy at the top of his head, which led to the Reiki healing system. He first used Reiki on himself, then tried it on his family. Since it worked well for various ailments, he decided to share this knowledge with the public at large. He opened a clinic in Harajuku, Aoyama— Tokyo—in April of the 10th year of the Taisho period (in 1921). He not only gave treatment to countless patients, some of whom had come from far and wide, but he also hosted workshops to spread his knowledge. In September of the twelfth year of the Taisho period (1923), the devastating Kanto earthquake shook Tokyo. Thousands were killed, injured, or became sick in its aftermath. Dr. Usui grieved for his people, but he also took Reiki to the devastated city and used its healing powers on the surviving victims. His clinic soon became too small to handle the throng of patients, so in February of the 14th year of the Taisho period (1925), he built a new one outside Tokyo in Nakano.

His fame spread quickly all over Japan, and invitations to distant towns and villages started coming in. Once he went to Kure, another time to Hiroshima prefecture, then to Saga prefecture and Fukuyama.

It was during his stay in Fukuyama that he was hit by a fatal stroke on March 9th, of the fifteenth year of the Taisho period (1926). He was 62 years of age.

Dr. Usui had a wife named Sadako; her maiden name was Suzuki. They had a son and a daughter. The son, Fuji Usui took over the family business after Dr. Usui's passing.

Dr. Usui was a very warm, simple and humble person. He was physically healthy and well-proportioned. He never showed off and always had a smile on his face; he was also very courageous in the face of adversity. He was, at the same time, a very cautious person. His talents were many. He liked to read, and his knowledge of medicine, psychology, fortune-telling and theology of religions around the world was vast. This life-long habit of studying and gathering information certainly helped pave the way to perceiving and understanding Reiki. Reiki not only heals diseases, but also amplifies innate abilities, balances the spirit, makes the body healthy, and thus helps achieve happiness. To teach this to others you should follow the five principles of the Meiji Emperor and contemplate them in your heart.

They should be spoken daily, once in the morning and once in the evening.

          1) Don't get angry today.
          2) Don't worry today.
          3) Be grateful today.
          4) Work hard today.
          5) Be kind to others today.

The ultimate goal is to understand the ancient secret method of gaining happiness (Reiki) and thereby discover an all-purpose cure for many ailments. If these principles are followed you will achieve the great tranquil mind of the ancient sages. To begin spreading the Reiki system, it is important to start from a place close to you, don't start from something distant such as philosophy or logic.

Sit still and in silence every morning and every evening with your hands folded in the "Ghasso" or "Namaste". Follow the great principles, and be clean and quiet. Work on your heart and do things from the quiet space inside of you. Anyone can access Reiki, because it begins within yourself!

Philosophical paradigms are changing the world round. If Reiki can be spread throughout the world it will touch the human heart and the morals of society. It will be helpful for many people, and will not only heal disease but also the Earth as a whole. Over 2000 people learned Reiki from Dr. Usui. More learned it from his senior disciples, and they carried Reiki even further. Even now after Dr. Usui's passing, Reiki will spread far and wide for a long time to come. It is a universal blessing to have received Reiki from Dr. Usui and to be able to pass it on to others. Many of Dr.

Usui's students converged to build this memorial here at Saihoji Temple in the Toyotoma district.

I was asked to write these words to help keep his great work alive. I deeply appreciate his work and I would like to say to all of his disciples that I am honored to have been chosen for this task. May many understand what a great service Dr. Usui did to the world.

As the memorial stone explains, Dr. Usui was on retreat at a Buddhist monastery outside Kyoto on Mt. Kurama when he discovered Reiki. He had been fasting for 21 days when he felt a powerful energy descending upon his head, and his understanding of the Reiki healing system was born.

Dr. Usui chose to accept the new pathway laid before him in that moment of illumination. He was deeply changed, and his transformation affected many people for decades to come; it continues to do so. Had he been a Christian, Dr. Usui might have described his new vocation as working to further God's healing mission on earth, so that humankind can more fully experience the indwelling Kingdom of God. In the language of his own Buddhist understanding, Dr. Usui surely felt blessed that, through the gift of Reiki, he could help eliminate suffering in the world.

The Handbook of Dr. Usui

For the past couple of decades, significant new information about Dr. Usui has come—and continues to come—to light. One of the most notable recent discoveries is the *Reiki Healing Method Handbook* (the *Reiki Ryoho Hikkei*) which Dr. Usui purportedly gave out to his Shoden (First Degree) students. Many believe that this handbook was put together by Chujiro Hayashi, at Dr. Usui's request.

Working from previously known material, the late Kimiko Koyama, sixth president of the Japanese Usui Reiki Ryoho Gakkai (the Usui Spiritual Energy Healing Association) recreated the handbook for the group's fiftieth anniversary in the late 20th century. It would be inaccurate to say that Dr. Usui compiled the manual as we now have it, since the handbook was given its final form through the editorial work of Ms. Koyama, and it includes both information from Dr. Hayashi (a medical doctor and one of Mikao Usui's most influential students) as well as 125 poems (gyosei) composed by the Meiji Emperor of Japan.[6]

Nonetheless, Mikao Usui's influence and voice echo throughout the book, particularly in the Introduction, which was written by him, and in the Question and Answer section, in which he is interviewed.[7] It is moving to read, in his own words, his beliefs about the Reiki healing method, and his hopes and generous intentions for its proliferation.

The Introduction is reprinted in full below with permission of Frank Arjava Petter and Lotus Light Publications. Dr. Usui explains the spiritual energy that is Reiki.

From time immemorial, it has often happened that someone who has found an original, secret law has either kept it for himself or only shared it with his descendents (sic).

This secret was then used as security in life for his descendents. The secret is not passed on to outsiders. However, this is an old-fashioned custom from the last century.

In times like these, the happiness of humanity is based on working together and the desire for social progress.

This is why I would never allow anyone to possess it just for himself!

Our Reiki Ryoho is something absolutely original and cannot be compared with any other path in the world.

This is why I would like to make this method available to the public for the well-being of humanity. Each of us has the potential of being given a gift by the divine, which results in the body and soul becoming unified. In this way, a great many people will experience the blessing of the divine.

First of all, our Reiki Ryoho is an original therapy, which is built upon the spiritual power of the universe.

Through it, the human being will first be made healthy, and then peace of mind and joy in life will be increased.

Today we need improvements and restructuring in our lives so that we can free our fellow human beings from illness and emotional suffering.

This is the reason why I dare to freely teach this method in public.[8]

Dr. Chujiro Hayashi and Mrs. Hawayo Takata

I have mentioned that one of Mikao Usui's foremost students was Dr. Chujiro Hayashi, a medical doctor and retired naval admiral. Apparently at Dr. Usui's suggestion, Hayashi opened his own Reiki clinic, still with close ties to the Usui Reiki Ryoho Gakkai.[9] But by 1931, five years after Dr. Usui's death, Dr. Hayashi began to develop his own branch of Reiki. Four years later, in 1935, it was to Dr. Hayashi's clinic that Mrs. Hawayo Takata would come, seeking help for her many ailments.

Mrs. Takata had traveled from her home in Hawaii to her native Japan, in order to deliver to her parents the sad news of the death of her sister, one of their daughters. While in Japan she entered a hospital and was diagnosed with a tumor, gallstones, appendicitis and asthma. Surgery was recommended, but at the last moment she chose instead to visit Dr. Hayashi's Reiki clinic in Tokyo. Four months later she was completely healed, and enthusiastically began to study Reiki with Dr. Hayashi.

In February of 1938, after three years of study, Hawayo Takata became one of only 13 Reiki masters Chujiro Hayashi trained in his lifetime. She then brought Dr. Hayashi's adapted style of Usui Reiki, via Hawaii, to the U. S. mainland, traveling, teaching and healing extensively. Before her death in 1980, Mrs. Takata had trained 22 Reiki masters.[10] These include her granddaughter Phyllis Lei Furumoto, who is honored by the Reiki Alliance as the Grandmaster of Reiki.

As Mrs. Takata continued to teach and practice Reiki, she found—as had Dr. Hayashi before her—that some adjustments to the original Usui system would be helpful. John Gray, one of the 22 Masters she created, writes that:

Reiki as Mrs. Takata learned it from Dr. Hayashi was too complicated and repetitive....She found that if she channeled energy with a series of hand placements covering key points in certain patterns on the body, it worked as well as the complex approach Hayashi had documented. Takata combined many of the hand positions found in Dr. Hayashi's manual, standardizing the patterns so that every Reiki treatment would be the same. In this way she created what she called a "foundation treatment," making the system much easier to learn. This was her genius and one of her major contributions to Reiki.[11]

Since Mrs. Takata's death in 1980 there have been many developments in the teaching of Reiki. New hand positions, symbols and techniques have appeared, and currently a great variety of Reiki methods—most very recognizable adaptations of the original Usui method—are taught throughout the world.

Such a plethora of options can sometimes be confusing, but it also offers a veritable banquet of choices and an enormous amount of healing energy. Still, it is wise to be sure you have been fully informed regarding the curriculum of any Reiki class—and the credentials of any Reiki teacher—before you sign up. (See Chapter Four: Finding a Teacher and Choosing a Class)

Reiki Today: The Story Continues

The Usui Reiki Ryoho Gakkai (founded by Dr. Usui in 1922) is still active in Japan. The group has had seven presidents to date, the first being Mikao Usui. The current president is Masaki Kondo, a university professor.

Once there were 80 branches of the group throughout Japan, but now there are five. The primary teaching meetings take place in Tokyo. Mr. Hiroshi Doi is the only member of the society who has spoken to the West about Reiki, and I recommend his book *Modern Reiki Method for Healing* to those interested in Reiki as it is currently practiced in Japan.[12] Sadly, because the book is out of print a used copy is rather costly.

In addition to the Japanese Reiki school, there are a great many Reiki teachers of note practicing in the West. Walter Lubeck,

Pamela Miles, Frank Arjava Petter, William Lee Rand, Bronwen and Frans Stiene are but a few. Based in various countries, these master instructors travel around the world sharing the good news of Reiki; you can either travel to them or wait until they come to your area. Simply Google their names and schedules for more information.

Dr. Usui wrote that he shared the gift of Reiki with the world for the wellbeing of humanity, so that "a great many people will experience the blessing of the divine."[13] Thanks be to God for the wisdom and generosity Mikao Usui showed in sharing this spiritual healing path with us.

REIKI, MEDICINE & SCIENCE

CHAPTER THREE

The Basics

Reiki (pronounced RAY-kee) is a Japanese word. The first syllable, "rei" translates as "spiritual, " "divine," or "universal." The second syllable, "ki" means "energy. Taken together, the syllables mean "divine energy" or "spiritual energy," often known in Christianity as the Holy Spirit, i.e. the Spirit of God or even the breath of God. This energy or Spirit manifests itself physically by flowing through the body along systems of energy conduits such as chakras, meridians and pressure points.

We know from quantum physics that everything in the universe is made up of constantly moving energy. Even things that seem solid, like cars, furniture, or rocks, are in unceasing motion, although the energy runs at speeds undetectable to the naked eye. Christians believe that this energy, which makes up all things, flows from God, who is the Source of all. Therefore, the healing possibilities this divine energy (literally "Reiki") offers are gifts from our Creator.

Healing touch is an accepted part of the Christian tradition. Jesus fully manifested the divine power which is available to us all, and he shared that power through speech, miraculous acts of loving kindness, and also through the laying on of hands. Thus, Reiki healing fits easily into traditional Christian practice, since it involves both the laying on of hands, and the utilization of spiritual energy.

During a Reiki healing session, the practitioner draws on the divine energy which saturates both the universe around us and our own body systems. This spiritual energy (Reiki) is then channeled into the recipient. The freshly infused energy relieves blockages in the receiver's energetic systems, and the body's natural healing processes are encouraged. Wellbeing and health are promoted, and energetic imbalances—which weaken our ımune systems and make us susceptible to dis-ease—are iscouraged.

As Reiki flows into the recipient it "is controlled not by the practitioner, but rather by the natural needs of the patient or client who is receiving....When people are in good health, they draw little energy....When the need is great, the flow is very powerful and both practitioner and client will notice it.[14]

Reiki and Western Medicine

The traditional Western approach to medicine is effective and life-giving, but tends to be skewed toward symptom relief, rather than investigation of cause and prevention. Drugs, often prohibitively expensive, are so widely prescribed that patients half seriously speculate that their doctors are in the pockets of the pharmaceutical companies. Dr. Christiane Northrup, the well-known gynecologist/obstetrician, jokes that a woman suffering from chronic yeast infections is often treated as though she has a Monistat deficiency.[15]

We all know that prescription drugs can have very toxic side effects. When two or more of these medicines are mixed, the negative effects may increase exponentially, causing body harmony to spin out of control and ending by making the cure worse than the disease.

Invasive procedures that violate and traumatize the body on many levels are a standard part of medical practice in the West. Most of us know people for whom surgery was a great blessing—but we also probably know people for whom it proved not only unhelpful, but harmful or even fatal.

Notwithstanding its drawbacks, Western medicine is a great boon. People around the globe have benefited from our scientific research and the resultant medicines and procedures. No health care system in the world offers more hope or better results when swift and incisive medical intervention is needed.

Yet the benefits offered by energetic healing methods such as Reiki should not be undervalued. Many in the Western medical community now recognize the value of stimulating the body's own healing abilities through methods such as Reiki, methods that are

28

blessedly free from negative side effects. Even better, Reiki simple to learn and, when practiced regularly, can harmonize whole body, preventing manifestation of physical dis-ease.

More and more people are turning to complementary healing techniques, including medical professionals who are integrating energetic healing into their practices. I have taught Reiki to a number of doctors, nurses, and health care chaplains. Many hospitals now offer Reiki training and/or Reiki sessions to both patients and staff, while Reiki and other healing touch methods are often found in the curricula at teaching hospitals—a hopeful sign.

The Yale-New Haven Hospital website offers this explanation of Reiki: "Reiki is a Japanese word meaning 'Universal Life Energy.' The practice of Reiki is a non-intrusive method of hands-on healing. During a Reiki session, healing energy lulls you into a deeply relaxed state. It is this deep relaxation that increases energy as the body rests and becomes revitalized during the session. Our Reiki practitioners are trained and certified by master-level Reiki teachers."[16]

Hartford Hospital's website offers a thorough explanation of its Reiki menu, and includes patient feedback such as the following: "This was a wonderful part of my stay at Hartford Hospital. The Reiki sessions I received were the highlight of my day. It is super that this is being offered to patients. Keep it up!"[17]

Memorial Sloan-Kettering Hospital in New York City has a wide menu of complementary therapies, including acupuncture, massage, meditation, reflexology, self-hypnosis, and Reiki. The hospital website explains that, "Reiki promotes the healing of physical and emotional ailments through gentle touch. Reiki consists of gentle, hands-on healing techniques for restoring harmony and providing deep relaxation and a sense of clarity."[18]

The number of hospitals now offering Reiki is impressive. To get more specific information, you can go to The Center for Reiki Research. The Center has a list of hospitals offering Reiki, although you will need to become a member (free) to gain access to the list. Alternatively, you can simply go to the websites of hospitals near you. There is a good chance that they will offer Reiki, since four years ago over 800 hospitals already offered Reiki, and that number continues to grow.[19]

I do not mean to minimize the efficacy of traditional Western medicine. Without surgical techniques, chemotherapy, or even antibiotics, I might not be alive. But we in the West are also discovering how effective energetic healing systems can be in the pursuit of wellness—and without unfortunate drug side effects and/or painful, invasive and expensive procedures.

Energetic healing methods are truly complementary; they can be used in conjunction with traditional medical approaches. And there is even better news: healing practices like Reiki are preventive, and by faithfully utilizing these simple hands-on techniques, you can help keep your doctor's waiting room a bit less crowded!

Reiki and Eastern Medicine

As you have probably inferred, the Eastern approach to health care is primarily energy-centered, rooted in the belief that balanced energy positively affects the whole body, eradicating dis-ease and its attendant symptoms at the source. There is an ancient Chinese saying: "There is no pain if there is a free flow of Qi; if there is pain, there is no free flow of Qi." ("Qi" being the Chinese equivalent of the Japanese "Ki"; both mean "energy.")

Reiki and other energy healing methods offer our disharmonized modern bodies an energetic boost. Eastern practitioners understand that this helps clear our energy pathways, restoring our whole beings to their intended states of balance and strength.

Energetic healing is widespread in Eastern Asia, where medical professionals consider techniques such as acupuncture, herbal medicine, and various forms of healing touch—including Reiki—to be primary defenses against dis-ease. In the West, even where these methods are available, they are rarely regarded as first choice options against health challenges. In fact, such healing methods are often labeled "alternative" rather than "complementary"—the former term erroneously implying a mutual exclusivity between energy medicine and traditional medicine. Still, this attitude is slowly changing, and we can hope that in the not-too-distant future more insurance companies will support their policyholders should they choose to visit their Reiki, massage, or chiropractic practitioners, rather than—or in addition to—their medical doctors.

Reiki and Emotional Healing

We are learning that the relationship between body, mind and spirit is less a connection, and more an inseparable union. It follows that Reiki, so effective in situations of physical dis-ease, is equally effective in cases of mental, emotional or spiritual imbalance.

I have experienced firsthand Reiki's positive impact on volatile emotions. I have always been a person of mercurial emotions, but when I began practicing Reiki self-healing, over a period of several months I noticed that my emotional shifts became less pronounced, and troubling feelings passed off more easily. Over time my emotions have continued to grow more peaceful, and I have gained in confidence and clarity. Apparently when one's energy systems are flowing freely it is harder for troubling emotional states to linger.

In her book, *Reiki: A Comprehensive Guide*, Pamela Miles cites a study examining the effects of Reiki on depression. In the study, people who scored high on standard depression scales received six weeks of Reiki sessions, and improved significantly more than others who received six weeks of placebo sessions from "unqualified" (i.e., untrained) practitioners. Encouragingly, follow-up tests a year later showed that the benefits lasted, although no additional Reiki was offered.

A third group in this same study was given "distant Reiki," a technique in which the healing energy is sent to someone in another location. (Think healing prayer.) Remarkably, the group receiving Reiki from a distance showed improvement equal to that displayed by those who had received hands-on Reiki.[20] This is a telling reminder that the movements of God's Holy Spirit (i.e. spiritual energy) are unlimited by time and space. Christians have always known this, of course; it is why we pray for people and situations not in our immediate physical vicinity. Distant Reiki is simply a form of healing prayer.

Although Reiki has tended to be primarily associated with physical healing, stabilization of one's mental, emotional and spiritual balance can be quite remarkable. Reiki positively affects the whole being.

Reiki and Science

Studies such as the one cited in Pamela Miles' book are rapidly accumulating, and are readily available on the Internet, in Reiki books, and in periodicals such as William Lee Rand's excellent *Reiki News Magazine*. Although these resources, together with the personal experience of thousands of people, offer impressive evidence that Reiki is effective, they can hardly be considered scientific proof. The question remains, is there any way to satisfactorily and scientifically explain how Reiki works?

Due to the growth of interest in energy medicine, many distinguished scientists now have ideas and information to offer in response to this question.

Early in the twentieth century Albert Einstein demonstrated that matter and energy are interchangeable ($E=MC^2$). Scientists are still working to grasp all the implications of that equation, and they continue to explore the nature of reality through the theories of relativity, quantum physics, superstrings, etc. Such theories claim that matter and energy are woven into a single unified field. In other words, all is connected, and all is in dynamic flux.[21]

One of the many results of these shifting understandings has been to provide a foundation for more deeply exploring energy medicine. James Oschman, PhD, is a cellular biologist and physiologist who has been one of the leaders in this field. Dr. Oschman has degrees in Biophysics and Biology, and has worked in major research labs around the world, including those at Cambridge University, the University of Copenhagen, and Northwestern University. In his books *Energy Medicine: the Scientific Basis*, and *Energy Medicine in Therapeutics and Human Performance*, he "gives the most skeptical academic scientists a theoretical basis for exploring the physiology and biophysics of energy medicines."[22]

During his investigations, Dr. Oschman associated with Rolfers, Reiki practitioners, acupuncturists, and other body workers; all people who work against a backdrop of public misinformation and doubt, if not actual disdain. His findings, and those of other modern researchers, tell a biological and scientific story that coincides with the daily experiences of energy therapists ranging from medical doctors taking advantage of PEMF techniques, to acupuncturists, to polarity therapists, Reiki practitioners, herbalists, aromatherapists and so on.[23]

In *Energy Medicine: The Scientific Basis* Dr. Oschman relates the historical travails of one Franz Anton Mesmer, an eighteenth century physician and one of the earliest proponents of magnetic therapy. Mesmer discovered "unusual currents coursing through his patients' bodies prior to the onset of a 'healing crisis' that led to a cure." He soon realized "that he could produce the same phenomena without the magnets, simply by passing his hands above the patient's body." Sadly, when invited to witness Mesmer's very popular work, the scientists of the day predictably responded with "ridicule, animosity, malicious rumours, slander, and fear." Nevertheless, time has vindicated his beliefs.[24]

Dr. Oschman saw a clear relationship between Mesmer's method and "the laying on of hands used by Jesus and other religious figures. Modern methods resembling that of Mesmer include therapeutic touch, polarity therapy, Reiki, aura balancing, and many others. A variety of clinical trials have shown the efficacy of these methods, and...research has begun to explain how they are effective."[25]

As he studied and observed, "Oschman noted similarities between the frequencies and intensities of low energy emissions from the hands of therapists and the signals from the pulsed electromagnetic field (PEMF) devices used in clinical medicine." He postulated that polarity therapy, the Reiki healing method, therapeutic touch, acupuncture, and many other hands-on therapies probably affect the same signal pathways in comparable ways.[26]

Ultimately, Dr. Oschman came to the revolutionary but well-evidenced understanding that the human body acts as a liquid crystal, vibrating at many different frequencies. He moved from this realization to the discovery, borne out by research, that pulsing energetic vibrations—whether offered through a PEMF device or through the biomagnetic field emanating from a therapist's hands—can positively affect the body's own vibrations.

"Scientific consensus has gone from a certainty that weak environmental energies can have no influence on living systems to agreement that such influences are extremely important and deserving of intense study to determine the precise mechanisms involved." These new concepts do not ask that we abandon our sophisticated scientific understandings of physiology, biochemistry or molecular biology. Instead, they extend our picture of living processes, and of healing.[27]

Candace B. Pert., Ph.D., is another scientist of note who has been open to exploration of the mind-body-spirit unity, and who believes that "reductionist Cartesian thought is now in the process of adding something very new and exciting—and holistic."[28] Dr. Pert is a former research professor of Physiology and Biophysics from Georgetown University Medical Center, and an internationally renowned neuroscientist and pharmacologist with a degree from Johns Hopkins University. She held a number of research positions with the National Institute of Health after 1975, and she served as Chief of the Section on Brain Biochemistry of the Clinical Neuroscience Branch of the NIMH until 1987. She is famed for her discovery of the opiate receptor, the cellular binding site for endorphins in the brain.[29]

Dr. Pert has lectured worldwide in these and other areas, including her theories on emotions and mind-body communication. She appeared as one of the experts in Bill Moyers' 1993 PBS video production, *Healing and the Mind*, and in the 2004 film *What the #$*! Do We Know!?*. She was featured in *The Washingtonian* magazine in 2001 as one of Washington's 50 "Best and Brightest" individuals.[30] Her popular book, *Molecules of Emotion, Why You Feel the Way You Feel* expounds on her research and theories.[31]

Dr. Pert points out that science, of necessity, moves slowly in order to avoid making huge mistakes, but that eventually "the new view becomes the status quo....which is what is happening today as a new paradigm comes into being." Largely, Pert claims, through the efforts of the "holistic/alternative healthy crowd...such formerly dismissed techniques as acupuncture and hypnosis have gained the credibility they now have."[32]

During an interview for *Healing and the Mind*, Pert told Moyers that

I personally think there are many phenomena that we can't explain without going into energy. As a scientist, I believe that we're going to understand everything one day, but that this understanding will require bringing in a realm we don't understand at all yet. We're going to have to bring in that extra-energy realm, the realm of spirit and soul that Descartes kicked out of Western scientific thought. [33]

In her book, *Molecules of Emotion*, Pert explains that

...because of the growing public awareness of my research on endorphins and other neuropeptides, people from all kinds of unexpected backgrounds...sought me out....A bearded yogi dressed in white and wearing a turban showed up at my office one day to ask me if endorphins were concentrated along the spine in a way that corresponded to the Hindu chakras. The chakras, he explained were centers of 'subtle energy' that governed basic physical and metaphysical functions from sexuality to higher consciousness. I had no idea what he was talking about, but, trying to be helpful, I pulled out a diagram that depicted how there were two chains of nerve bundles located on either side of the spinal cord, each rich with many of the information-carrying peptides. He placed his own chakra map over my drawing and together we saw how the two systems overlapped. It was the first time I seriously considered that there might be a connection between my work and the Eastern viewpoint. Before he left, the yogi taught me some simple exercises for focusing attention at each of the chakra levels, which I

experimented with and found highly enjoyable for the
energizing effects they produced.[34]

Although our scientific knowledge is constantly growing, there is much about the body that we do not yet fully understand. Healing miracles—i.e., unexplained cures, referred to by medical science as "spontaneous remissions"—happen on a regular basis. These offer both a dramatic indication of how powerful is the body's potential for recovery from even the most devastating illness, as well as a humbling reminder of our lack of full understanding about the nature of our own beings.

Rational explanations are good things to have, and we are making great strides in understanding the way energy medicine works. However, although energetic medicine is being used more frequently in clinical settings through hands-on techniques, MRIs, PEMF devices, etc., we who practice complementary energetic methods such as Reiki, acupuncture, or massage, too often remain unaware that there is indeed a scientific basis for what we do. This lack of awareness is quite unfortunate, since understanding the physical mechanics underlying our practices can greatly increase our effectiveness.

The inability of energy therapists to explain our work in scientific terms means that groups like the Roman Catholic Bishops' Committee on Doctrine can make unchallenged, uninformed and erroneous statements such as the following: "Reputable scientific studies attesting to the efficacy of Reiki are lacking, as is a plausible scientific explanation as to how it could possibly be efficacious.[35] I am not sure what studies or documents the Bishops perused, but clearly they missed some significant ones.

In the end, rather than blaming those who are still unaware of the growing scientific consensus surrounding energy medicine, we who are practitioners must take the responsibility to educate ourselves in this area, so that we can offer informed and helpful responses to mistaken assumptions.

Until such time as the scientific understanding behind energy medicine is more widely understood and disseminated, we practitioners of these methods stand where we have traditionally stood: inviting those who are open to receiving Reiki to experience its healing benefits for themselves. For many, first-hand experience is as sufficient an explanation as any that scientific knowledge might offer. For those who prefer a more clinical and rational approach, the books referred to in this chapter provide an excellent beginning point for study.

The Future Of Reiki and Medicine

"By 1997, nearly half the American population was using complementary and alternative medicine (CAM), and using it a lot. That year, Americans made 629 million visits to CAM practitioners, more visits than they made to primary-care doctors." [36] The National Institutes of Health (NIH) responded to this statistic by creating the

National Center for Complementary and Alternative Medicine (NCCAM), a center devoted to studying these 'nonscientific' approaches to healing in order to understand if, when, and how they work, and whether they are safe....NCCAM makes that research available both to the public and the medical profession, so that effective CAM therapies can be integrated into conventional health care. The government is interested in CAM because it offers not only the promise of greater knowledge of prevention but also safer, less invasive treatments for many medical problems, and such benefits as faster recovery, shorter hospital stays, greater patient and staff satisfaction, and lower costs. [37]

My Perspective

I have seen the healing touch of Reiki work wonders in the rejuvenation of the body, mind and spirit—sometimes in situations that traditional Western medicine had failed to relieve. Moreover, we are now beginning to arrive at a scientific understanding of why Reiki and other complementary energetic methods may be so effective. This is very good news for all of us.

The gospel of Luke relates that Jesus commissioned the disciples and seventy elders to go out among the people and offer healing in the name of the Lord. Why would we, his contemporary followers, hesitate to follow that example? Reiki is a wonderful, specific and effective form of healing prayer, easily learned and readily accessible. The fruits of such a ministry are healing, loving kindness and wholeness. And now there are even scientific explanations (understood by believers to be rooted in God as Source of all) available to us.

Good news indeed!

LEARNING & PRACTICING REIKI

CHAPTER FOUR

In the Beginning

Since energy itself is always moving, it seems appropriate that the teaching of Reiki over the past century is a story of flexibility and adaptation. Even in the earliest days, Dr. Usui made a number of changes in his educational approach as he gained experience in teaching and practicing.

Becoming a Reiki practitioner was an intensive process for Dr. Usui's students. They met weekly, and students had to demonstrate intuitive knowledge of healing in order to progress. Some did this quickly, though others took much longer before moving on. "In Japan the Reiki path is seen as a course of life that is followed through many decades to the end of a person's days. A student in Japan sometimes only attained the Second Reiki Degree after ten or twenty years of practice. And the majority of the students never achieved the higher levels. They were and always remained students."[38]

Dr. Usui was open to the exploration of other methods and philosophies in his pursuit of the most thorough and effective training. Dave King—speaking for Mariko Obaasan, one of Mikao Usui's original students—writes, "Resident speakers and guests often presented material from other spiritual and religious groups. There were at least five versions of the (Reiki) system during its six years of development" in the early 1920's.[39]

Dr. Usui eventually developed a curriculum which included training for particular levels of proficiency, plus transition rituals for students moving from one degree to the next. Martial arts terms were originally used for the differing levels, although today Western Usui Reiki utilizes only three levels: Reiki One, Reiki Two, and Master Level (Reiki Three)

Dr. Chujiro Hayashi, the naval medical doctor who would one day teach Mrs. Hawayo Takata, joined the group in the mid-1920's.

At Mikao Usui's request, Dr. Hayashi created a handbook for the students based on a more overtly medical approach than had originally been used.[40]

Mikao Usui named Dr. Hayashi as his successor, and when the former died in 1926, Hayashi became one of the leaders of the Reiki healing method in Japan. He opened his own clinic in the late 1920's. The clinic contained eight beds and employed 16 Reiki practitioners, who worked in pairs.[41] It was to this clinic that Hawayo Takata came for healing in 1935. She was so startled by the intense warmth pouring from the practitioners' hands that she tried to look up their kimono sleeves to see where they hid the heaters![42]

After Mikao Usui's death, Dr. Hayashi continued to refine the Reiki teaching method, editing the student handbook still further and introducing a slightly altered system of hand positions, which he passed on to his students, including Hawaya Takata.[43] She, in her turn, brought Hayashi's system to the West and further adapted it. Her hand positions, along with the Reiki Ideals, the attunement process and the Reiki symbols, form the foundation of Usui Reiki as it is commonly taught in the West today.

John Gray, a student of Hawayo Takata's, points out, "There has been a direct and specific line of development of Reiki techniques and teachings—hand to hand—from Mikao Usui to Chujiro Hayashi to Hawayo Takata. We feel blessed to be direct beneficiaries—from their hands to our hands—of their sacrifices, teachings, and insight."[44]

Finding a Teacher

Finding the right teacher is an important initial step in learning Reiki. Look for an instructor who is certified specifically in Usui Reiki, because there are many variations on the Reiki theme out there. Some have integrity, but others are far removed from Dr. Usui's teachings, so it's a good idea to check training and teaching credentials and ask for references.

Christians seeking Reiki training may wish to ask a prospective teacher about his or her understanding of Reiki as spiritual energy. Some instructors have a theological/philosophical approach to

Reiki that might be troubling to a Christian. Be open, and remember that Reiki is based in spirituality, not any specific religion. But be sensible as well, and look for a teacher who speaks your spiritual language. Otherwise, you may feel puzzled by the teacher's perspective, and doubt the trustworthiness of your instructor and your training.

Reiki is not the product of any particular religious persuasion, so it is a simple matter for any Reiki teacher to present it from a Christian perspective—or indeed from the perspective of any religious tradition. Through the use of appropriate meditations, stories and illustrations, the material easily adapts to the themes of healing, love and compassion found in all of the world's great religions.

Choosing a Class

Reiki teachers organize their classes in a variety of ways, but generally speaking instruction for Levels One and Two requires a minimum of five to eight hours of training per level, depending upon the size of the class. In addition, each one of the three sessions of Level Three (Master Level) normally takes five to eight hours. Cost of Level One is generally around $100-200; Level Two $200-400; Master Level $800-1500.

It is traditional to wait six to twelve months after Level One before beginning Level Two, and to let another six to twelve months elapse between Levels Two and Three. Despite this convention there are a number of well-known and excellent Usui Reiki teachers who offer multi-level classes in a single weekend— Levels One and Two combined is very common—and that approach is quite appealing in our fast-paced society.

These experienced instructors travel around the U.S. or abroad, and their classes are usually outstanding, offering great opportunities for students to meet other Reiki practitioners and to study with excellent teachers. Most of them teach from a broadly spiritual—though not specifically religious—perspective. As we know, Reiki is compatible with any religion but limited to none, which means that each student can bring his or her own spiritual/religious perspective into the class.

The downside of these Reiki courses—which include travel expenses plus class costs—is that they are inevitably more expensive than studying with a local teacher would be. The classes also tend to be fairly large, so students naturally cannot receive the individual attention offered in a smaller class. From my perspective travel classes work best for practitioners who are already grounded in Reiki and who wish to continue and expand their Reiki education.

Whatever educational environment you decide best fits your budget and learning style—and despite Reiki's overall simplicity—you can expect that in the short term all the new information coming your way will feel confusing and even overwhelming. Be assured that with patience, practice, and some time, your relationship with Reiki, as with any spiritual discipline, will steady and grow.

Reiki One: What to Expect

Because of my vocation as an Episcopal priest, I teach from the Christian perspective. However, on a number of occasions I have taught people of other faith traditions, and it has been a pleasure, not a difficulty.

First Degree Reiki emphasizes self-healing, for we must take care of ourselves in order to be effective in helping others. I believe it was the Dalai Lama who suggested that the best gift each of us can give to the world is a healthy self. I think Jesus would concur.

Out of genuine concern for the needs of others, many Christians (and no doubt people of other faiths) believe that caring for oneself is selfish. We forget that Jesus habitually withdrew from the crowds, seeking solitude and prayer, soaking in God's presence so he could carry on with God's mission of healing love. Rather than ignoring our own need for replenishment and relaxation, we should emulate Jesus' model for self-care; First Degree Reiki helps us do this.

My Level One students learn the origins and theory of Reiki; the guidelines and hand positions for self-healing; and how to offer "chair" Reiki to others. They are initiated into the energies of

Reiki four separate times during the class. (See Attunements section which follows)

Reiki fits into the Christian healing ministry in a number of ways—not least in the common intuitive understanding that, as we pray for someone, where we place our hands matters. Well-known Christian healer Agnes Sanford tells a delightful story that illustrates the importance of effective hand position.

> *Once I was called to see a baby girl ill with pneumonia. I knelt beside her crib in silence, **laid one hand upon the small, congested chest and slipped the other one beneath her back,** and asked God to come into her. Soon the waxy frame of the baby was filled with a visible inrushing of new life. Even the hands and feet vibrated, as if an electric current were entering into her. A look of tension on the tiny face was smoothed away and she passed from a semi-conscious condition into a natural sleep. Two hours later her doctor came into the room. He stopped at the threshold, eyes staring, jaw dropped in surprise. For he had come to report his hospital arrangements for the child and he beheld his small patient, bright-eyed and cheerful, sitting up in bed.*
>
> *"Mine doctor," said she, "can I have a cookie?"*
>
> *"My God!" exclaimed the doctor, startled out of his bedside manner. "What's happened to her?"*
>
> *He was quite right. It was his God who had intervened—that was what had happened to her.[45] (boldface added)*

At the end of Level One, students are certified as Reiki practitioners. They will have trained and practiced intensely, while immersed in a refreshing energetic environment; it is like spending the day soaking in prayer. Class members who arrived with headaches, pain or fatigue, will leave with their discomfort gone and a new sense of purpose and energy. In his book *A Beginner's Guide to Reiki,* David Vennells marvels that, "Nothing could have prepared me for First Degree Reiki. It was a complete revelation, a weekend that transformed my life."[46]

Reiki Two: Sharing Reiki with Others

Reiki Two continues the self-healing work begun in First Degree, and also prepares the student to offer Reiki to other people. With increased study and experience, the student's energetic abilities grow stronger and more reliable. Hawayo Takata described it thus: "First degree, 20 horsepower; Second degree, 100 horsepower—very powerful."[47] Or, as Agnes Sanford puts it, "Learning to live in the kingdom of Heaven is learning to turn on the light of God within...."[48] Like anything else, the more we practice the more effective we become.

During Level Two students will become familiar with the Reiki Ideals and will learn how to use the Level Two symbols (see following sections) Second degree graduates are certified to offer Reiki to the general public, whether as members of a church or other pastoral care ministry, in a private practice, a spa, or a medical/clinical environment.

During second degree each student is attuned once. However, if Level Two is taught in more than one class session, it makes sense to offer an attunement each time if possible. An attunement is a form of intense prayer, a soaking in God's presence and consciously asking for a strengthening of our ability to channel God's healing energies.

Students who complete Level Two are encouraged to wait six to twelve months before proceeding to Level Three (Master Level). This allows time for absorption of the new abilities and information; spiritual growth cannot be rushed. Still, there is no Reiki police force on the job, so each teacher and each student will need to decide upon an appropriate pace of study.

The Reiki Ideals (Level Two)

Dr. Usui did not himself write the Reiki Ideals (which are sometimes called Principles or Precepts). Rather, he borrowed them from writings of the Japanese Emperor Meiji (1852-1912), a leader concerned with developing healthy and considerate citizenship in his people. These roots go deep; even today in Japan courtesy and consideration for others are considered indispensable to the creation of a well-ordered society.

44

The Reiki Ideals are similar to the Twelve Steps, in that they offer a solid philosophical foundation for daily living. It makes sense for Reiki teachers to learn them well, and to encourage their students to do the same. I like to have my students memorize the Ideals, and they also receive laminated copies of them in bookmark form. They are an excellent addition to any daily devotion.

Below are the traditional Reiki Ideals, followed by an adapted version of them that I include in my personal prayer time. The adapted version is fluid and can be adjusted as needed. Consider creating your own version of the Ideals, which can address the ongoing challenges and gifts of your life.

The Original Reiki Ideals

Just for today—

1) Do not be angry.
2) Do not worry.
3) Be grateful.
4) Work diligently.
5) Be kind to people.

An Adaptation of the Ideals

Just for today, with the help of the Holy Spirit and the hosts of heaven, I will try to:

1) Be gently confident—not angry, arrogant or insecure;
2) Be peaceful—not anxious;
3) Be filled with gratitude—and not be of critical mind;
4) Fulfill my life's purpose diligently—and not be easily distracted;
5) Abide in compassion, forgiveness, loving kindness, openness, understanding and wisdom with all creation—including myself; striving ever toward a calm mind and a good heart.

A friend once asked why I have negative statements in my adaptation of the Ideals. I do this because otherwise I may forget to check for what Jesus referred to as the "speck" in the eye; what

Carl Jung called the shadow self. This inclusive version of the Ideals acknowledges, and accepts, my whole being.

The Reiki Symbols (Level Two)

Second Degree Reiki includes the teaching of the first three Reiki symbols. Much energy has been devoted to the "sacredness" and "secrecy" of these symbols, and these claims are excessive. Symbols themselves are not sacred. A symbol may point to that which is sacred, but to call the symbol itself sacred would be considered idolatry in the Christian system of belief, like worshipping a statue or an icon, rather than what it represents.

Our modern belief that the symbols should be kept secret stems partly from Hawayo Takata's teachings; her students were not allowed to keep copies of them. Yet ironically, in Japan the symbols are not considered secret. Some of them, in fact, are simply kanji (writing)—found in any Japanese dictionary.

I follow the traditional Western practice of not sharing the symbols with anyone uninitiated into Second Degree Reiki—not for any sacred or mystical reason, but out of respect for what I have been taught. Anyway, the symbols are meaningless to people who are unfamiliar with them.

In addition to its visual impact, each symbol has a sound component—a mantra, or particular energetic vibration. Although the use of sound/vibration is a valid healing technique, I confess that to date vocalizing the Reiki symbols has not moved me greatly. However, I am open to my own changing experience, and to the experience of others. Explore for yourself what impact the chanting of these mantras/symbols may have for you.

Each Reiki Two symbol has a particular meaning. Two are truly symbols—i.e., artistic representations of an idea. A third is simply a form of writing and can be found in the Japanese dictionary. Unfortunately, the emphasis on the symbols' secrecy and sacredness has encouraged people outside the Reiki community to believe there must be something darkly significant about them. This is untrue, for the symbols and their energy represent positive themes such as "harmony," "focus," and "connection"—nothing mysterious at all.

46

If you study Reiki, you will develop your own relationship with the symbols. Walter Lubeck's *The Big Book of Reiki Symbols*— Walter being one of the premier Reiki teachers on the planet—is a detailed resource for exploring the symbols and their possibilities.[49] You may find that you want to chant them daily, or visualize them as you give Reiki to yourself or others. Some practitioners find them extraordinarily powerful.

On the other hand, you may prefer the approach of Frank Arjava Petter—another renowned Reiki teacher—who feels that "Reiki symbols are tools to help us direct energy. Once you have learned to direct energy with the help of the symbols, I encourage you to let them go. After you have crossed the river you don't need to carry the ferryboat on your shoulders for the rest of your life!"[50]

Educate yourself in the meaning and use of the symbols, and let the place they will hold in your practice unfold naturally. Familiarity with them is essential for the well-trained Reiki practitioner; beyond that their use remains your own decision.

Reiki Three: ART and Master Level

Anyone wishing to become a Reiki master must complete all three classes of the Level Three (Master Level) training. Each of these classes typically runs from six to eight hours—depending on class size—totaling approximately 20 - 25 hours of in-class training.

The first of the Master level sessions is often called the ART (Advanced Reiki Training) class. This session is a requirement for prospective Reiki teachers, but can also be taken as a single class by Reiki Two practitioners who simply want to deepen their Reiki practice.

My ART students are introduced to a number of healing techniques: centering prayer/meditation; aromatherapy; the Japanese Reiki techniques; relief of pain through visualization; a few techniques taught (with permission) from Walter Lubeck's *Rainbow Reiki*; Jin Shin Jyutsu self-help; chakra healing methods; foot and hand reflexology; and the use of sound in healing. This is a great deal of material to cover, but it solidifies the student's Reiki foundation and provides new healing resources.

Students wishing to become Reiki teachers meet for two additional sessions, receiving a Master Level attunement each time. During classes they practice teaching the curriculum from Levels One and Two, they learn the three Master Symbols, and they spend considerable time giving Reiki to one another. All my Master students are required to give two Reiki sessions per week, and to keep a journal (which we discuss in class) documenting the sessions.

At the final class Master students learn to attune one another to all levels of Reiki. This is complicated and takes considerable time, but by the end of the class enough training will have been received to ensure the new graduates are well-qualified. If questions arise post-graduation, students are encouraged to seek clarification with me.

After Master level graduation students are traditionally called "Master Practitioners;" after they have taught their first class they become "Master Teachers."

Attunements

Attunements—or initiations—take place at each Reiki level, with minor alterations made to differentiate between the various degrees. The attunements are rituals during which the Reiki energy is formally passed from master to student, and the student opens up to become a more effective channel for the Reiki (divine energy).

I found the attunement process was the most troublesome aspect of learning Reiki. The student's eyes are closed during this time so I couldn't see what was going on, and that made me uncomfortable. In retrospect I should have asked for more information ahead of time. Remembering my own ignorance and resultant discomfort during attunement, I make sure to give my students an overview of what will be happening during that time. This frees them to enter into the spirit of the moment with openness and calm, rather than anxiety.

The various lineages of Usui Reiki offer different styles of attunement, although all involve the Usui Reiki symbols and the intentional passing of energy from Master to student through touch, visualization, thought and breath.

The use of the breath during attunements surprised me at first, but in fact the breath has ancient significance in healing and the giving of life. The Hebrew word "ruakh" translates as spirit, breath or wind—such as the Spirit of God (or the wind or breath of God) moving across the waters of creation, or God breathing the breath of life into Adam's nostrils in Genesis 2, or God breathing life into the dry bones in Ezekiel 37. Or, most significantly for us, Jesus breathing on the disciples and saying, "Receive the Holy Spirit." (John 20:22)

During an attunement the Christian Reiki teacher intentionally shares with the student an infusion of God's Holy Spirit (aka Reiki) which supports the student in becoming the most effective channel for that Spirit she can be. The echoes from the sacramental life of the church are obvious.

We know that God's energy is already present in all of us, as well as available all around us, and we trust that the attunement, plus our training, will help to clear us, opening our energetic channels wider so that we can more effectively share this spiritual energy with others.

There are many energetic healing methods in use today, and they work because God's energy is available to all. It is as though we intentionally plugged into an outlet that was already wired for electricity. In her book, *The Healing Light*, Agnes Sanford uses the plugging in of an iron to illustrate this availability of God's healing energy.

If we try turning on an electric iron and it does not work, we look to the wiring of the iron, the cord, or the house. We do not stand in dismay before the iron and cry, "Oh, electricity, please come into my iron and make it work!" We realize that while the whole world is full of that mysterious power we call electricity, only the amount that flows through the wiring of the iron will make the iron work for us. The same principle is true of the creative energy of God. The whole universe is full of it, but only the amount of it that flows through our own beings will work for us.[51]

Later in her book Sanford describes the ways in which our ability to channel God's energy can be blocked, and she suggests methods of living which maximize the flow of divine energy. As you might expect, these include regular prayer, intentionally practicing the presence of God, and living in the state of grace fostered through ongoing repentance, forgiveness and loving kindness.

Keeping our spirits in a state of health is as important as keeping our bodies healthy. When we attend to these matters faithfully, we will find it easier to "tap in" to the current of God's universal energy. The Reiki attunement is simply a formalized energetic pathway and ritual to help us do just that.

Practicing Reiki: The Reiki Session

Before using Reiki with people other than family and friends, a student should be certified in the first two levels. Again, the Reiki Police will not arrest you if you break this guideline, but it makes good sense to receive appropriate training before expanding your Reiki practice.

A traditional Reiki session takes place on a massage table, although Reiki is easily given to someone sitting in a chair, standing in a corner at a party, lying on a couch or in a hospital bed. The recipient is fully clothed. No lotions or potions are needed, though relaxing music can be played, lights can be slightly dimmed, temperature should be comfortable, etc., depending upon the wishes of the recipient and the practitioner.

It is customary but not necessary to lightly touch the body. In the case of rashes, insect bites and open wounds, the hands can be held just above the body. In some states only medical professionals, licensed massage therapists, and clerics may touch a person during a healing session, so check the laws in your area.

The practitioner prepares for the session by becoming still and aware of God's presence within and all around. Hopes for the session are mentally reviewed, and acceptance of God's greater intention for the person receiving is affirmed (i.e., we pray).

Work begins at the top of the head and moves down to the feet, covering major energy areas along the way, but never touching areas of the body that a (reasonably sized!) swimsuit would cover. The Christian practitioner continues to soak in prayer as she works, using the breath or the physical touch or some word or visualization as a mantra of healing.

Approximately 20 hand positions are used during a standard session—although most pastoral care sessions use fewer than that—and generally each position is held between one and three minutes. More time will be spent in areas where heat, cold, tingling or a magnetic pull is felt; areas that already feel balanced receive less time. By the end of a session, the recipient feels relaxed and nurtured; often people fall asleep. Please note that the energy will travel through the whole body even if the practitioner only lays a hand on the shoulder; it may take longer, but it will work.

A full session lasts approximately 60 minutes, and offers a compassionate and comforting time of sanctuary, which refreshes and soothes the spirit and the body, allowing them to do what God created them to do: to heal.

Practice Tips

There is a maxim that "a little Reiki is better than none at all." If you are a practitioner and you have only five minutes, use those few minutes and make them count, whether on yourself or someone else. "You can give yourself Reiki almost anywhere if you have a spare five or ten minutes....situations like traffic jams, before an interview, after an argument, and before or after any difficult situation."[52] Reiki is like prayer; generally the more time you have the better, but we know that God can and sometimes does work deeply in one amazing moment.

You will find many opportunities to use Reiki. You may find yourself at a gathering with someone who has a migraine headache or a sore shoulder. If the opportunity arises and the person is willing, take him aside for a few moments and silently— through prayer and touch—infuse fresh energy into the situation. It's lovely to have lots of time to prepare beforehand and lots of time to spend actually giving Reiki, but it simply does not always happen. This is why daily self-care is crucial: whenever you are called upon you will be in a reasonably balanced and effective state.

When using Reiki on children or pets, remember that their bodies process energy much more quickly than an adult's. They may turn away after only a few minutes, and this is a sign they have received all they need.

Although sometimes a result is immediately evident, generally Reiki (and other energetic healing methods including prayer) work subtly and over time. The rule of thumb is, the longer a particular condition has existed, the longer it may take to impact it. Just remember that some improvement will certainly be made in the short term, and perseverance will pay off in the long run.

We know healers at Dr. Hayashi's clinic worked in pairs or teams, and this is still a good option when possible, as it allows more energy to be transmitted more quickly. For this same reason Christians form prayer circles or groups; after all, Jesus commended it to us. "For where two or three are gathered in my name, I am there among them." (Matthew 18:20)

Forming a weekly or monthly Reiki Share or Reiki Circle, in which practitioners work in pairs or teams on one another, complements our daily self-care practice and also introduces us to other practitioners and the way they work. In addition to working on each other, such groups share their Reiki experiences, and together they send Reiki healing prayer to those in need.

There is no downside to using Reiki. There are no negative side effects and it complements any healing program. Moreover, while giving Reiki the practitioner benefits also, for God's energy flows through both giver and receiver. Win-win.

So-called miracles happen frequently around Reiki. Such incidents are especially impressive when traditional Western medicine has failed to help. Reiki is focused and powerful healing prayer; it allows us, as channels for the Spirit, to infuse fresh energy into a situation. What takes place after that is out of our hands—literally. We know that healing of some sort will always happen, but we cannot promise what form it will take.

Giving Reiki to someone who is terminally ill will not interfere with their passing; rather it can offer tranquility and comfort as they transition from this life to the next. A peaceful physical death is a form of healing, too—and who knows what marvelous healing awats us when we have passed beyond the limitations of this world? Be mindful of the needs of family members at these times, also. They too might receive great comfort from the Reiki touch, or include them in your prayers if touch seems inappropriate.

When we give ourselves and others Reiki, the energy of the Holy Spirit flows; it is a very specific and very effective form of healing prayer. Through it, our God-given energetic balance can be restored, compassion for ourselves and for others grows, and healing of the whole (holy) being flourishes. This is as great a blessing as any we could receive, for peace within each of us is the beginning of peace in the world.

REIKI & SCRIPTURE

CHAPTER FIVE

The Bible as Authority

The Holy Bible is the sacred Christian scripture, and its teachings are paramount when discussing Reiki and Christianity. As the contemporary followers of Christ, we recognize the importance of biblical authority for guidance in life issues.

Discernment in these matters is not straightforward, for although God remains immutable, historical contexts and human theological understandings do not. People and times change, and we are constantly learning and growing, through the ongoing revelation of the Holy Spirit. Consider the ways in which our lives differ—due to our own thoughtful and deliberate choices—from the ways in which our spiritual ancestors lived. If we followed common practice from biblical times, we might condone slavery, polygamy, animal sacrifice and stoning.

Though we have left behind many practices of our religious forebears, we have also added new ways of living they could not have imagined. The industrial and technological revolutions, explosive population growth, climate change and many other developments on our ever-shrinking yet ever-expanding planet were unforeseen by the most prophetic of our ancestors.

Consequently, when we turn to the Bible as authority, we view it—as did our forebears—from within our own historical and theological context. As a source wherein human beings have explored their relationship with and in God, and have exalted godly ways of living and being, the Bible's crucial guidance cannot be overstated. But using scripture as a specific, detailed rulebook for contemporary life is an exercise fraught with challenges.

Rather than treating biblical texts in a literal fashion, many Christians try to infer what Jesus might say or do in a particular situation. WWJD ("What Would Jesus Do") has entered our lexicon, and with good reason. We call to mind Christ's teachings on compassion, forgiveness, loving kindness and living more fully in the presence of God—aka bringing in the kingdom of God—and these great themes become our guideline and our lifeline. As for the inevitable gray areas, the places where we find ourselves genuinely unsure of the path God would have us walk—if we err, let us err on the side of generosity.

The healing touch of Reiki easily fits within the spirit and intention of holy scripture, especially as found in the gospels and pastoral letters, which chronicle the ministry of the early church. Jesus' God-given mission was to proclaim the good news of the Kingdom through the anointing of the Spirit of the Lord, and thereby to release captives, give sight to the blind, and free the oppressed; in other words, to restore wholeness to creation (Luke, 4:18-19). This mission he carried out through preaching, teaching, and healing, often through healing touch. As followers in Jesus' footsteps, we are invited to travel the pathway he trod before us.

Knowing the Texts

A foundational knowledge of scripture is crucial for all Christians, and Christian Reiki practitioners are no exception. We need a working familiarity with our sacred texts in order to make mature theological decisions about our faith and how we live it.

If you feel the need to amplify your biblical education (and who doesn't?) you might begin by purchasing a good annotated Bible and reading a chapter or two daily. You can begin with the New Testament if systematic Bible reading is new to you. Consider joining a church-sponsored Bible study, for the Bible is a very complex book (actually a collection of many small books). Excellent commentaries are available should you want deeper guidance than your study Bible offers: Eerdman's, Nelson's, Oxford, Strong's, or Zondervan, for example. Choose one that feels like a good fit for you.

If you are already a Reiki practitioner, consider including both the Lord's Prayer and the Reiki Ideals in your daily quiet time. When you make scripture reading and prayer a regular part of most days, your rapid growth will provide ample motivation to keep you on your consciously spiritual path.

The Old Testament

The Christian Bible begins with the books of the Old Testament (the Jewish scriptures) and tells the story of the Israelites, as expressed through the Law (the Torah, i.e. Genesis through Deuteronomy); the Writings (including Proverbs, the Psalms and selected others); and the Prophets (major and minor). The Israelites traced their relationship with the One God through the Patriarch Abraham, and the Old Testament illustrates how they understood the development of that relationship over time. Because the Jews are our spiritual ancestors, their history is foundational to our Christian story.

The Old Testament developed into its current form in the 1200 to 1500 years before Christ. Rooted in the oral tradition, over time the texts were written down and adapted by various editors (redactors) whose work expressed their particular theological viewpoints. These viewpoints naturally grew out of each editor's historical context, and how each saw God being revealed through that context.

The tale of the Israelites' exodus from Egypt, their journey into the Promised Land, their kings and kingdoms, their exile from and restoration to their homeland—all of it is the story of Divine Love so deep that it never falters, even in the face of shocking transgression or outright rejection. Set amid human violence and struggle, this is the story of a Love so powerful, so creative and so healing, that again and again new life for God's people arises from the ashes of failure and despair. From golden calves to Sodom and Gomorrah, through the thundering voices of the prophets calling the people to return to the Lord, in the despairing, humble yearning of the exiles for their home—God is there, unflagging, unchanging, understanding.

> *I, I am he who comforts you....You have forgotten the Lord, your Maker, who stretched out the heavens and laid the foundations of the earth....I have put my words in your mouth, and hidden you in the shadow of my hand, stretching out the heavens and laying the foundations of the earth, and saying to Zion, "You are my people." (Isaiah 51:12a; 13a; 16)*

God continually calls his beloved people beyond themselves into awareness, guiding them to offer others the same loving kindness and understanding they themselves have received. Although we often view the "Old Testament God" as harsh and judging, such gentle and lovely passages as the following are also a part of God's Old Testament voice; they still speak comfort and healing to our hearts.

He has told you, O mortal, what is good; and what does the Lord require of you but to do justice, and to love kindness, and to walk humbly with your God? (Micah 6:8)

Thus says the LORD, the God of your ancestor David: "I have heard your prayer, I have seen your tears; indeed, I will heal you...." (2 Kings 20:5b)

The New Testament

The New Testament continues the love story between God and God's people, manifested through the life, death, resurrection and ascension of Jesus of Nazareth. The gospel tales are followed by the books chronicling the establishment of the early Church, formed in Christ's name to pursue God's mission on earth: The Acts of the Apostles, the Epistles, the Pastoral Letters, and The Revelation to John. God sends Jesus to save (*diasozo*, also meaning to heal) not only the Jews, but the whole world.

Gone are the shocking Old Testament stories of supposedly God-sanctioned violence. The New Testament, through the figure of Jesus Christ, reveals God's nature as filled with grace and love.

And the Word became flesh and lived among us, and we have seen his glory, as of a father's only son, full of grace and truth....From his fullness we have all received, grace upon grace. The law indeed was given through Moses; grace and truth came through Jesus Christ. No one has ever seen God. It is God the only Son, who is close to the Father's heart, who has made him known. (John 1:14, 16-18)

Such is the marvelous journey to which we are called. In the face of Jesus Christ, Christians glimpse a healing Love so deep and broad that it defies our human comprehension.

As Christian Reiki practitioners we are also called; called to become effective members of the Christian healing ministry, embodying in this world the healing spirit of Christ.

Scripture and Healing

I suspect, though I have never actually counted, that the Old Testament contains more stories of battle than stories of healing. The Israelites believed in the mighty power of God, their great general who could ensure triumph in military engagements. When God, through Moses and Aaron, calls the people to leave Egypt and pass through the wilderness into the Promised Land, their very survival depends on trusting that the Lord their God is the mightiest warrior of all.

The New Testament might have unfolded more like the Old Testament if Jesus had been a Messiah in the style the Jews expected; i.e., a Zealot, burning to overthrow the hated Roman occupation. But instead of military conflict, the gospels tell stories of Christ preaching, teaching and healing all over the countryside; God's mission in action. Jesus mediates God's powerful healing/salvation to all people, guiding them toward the new Promised Land—i.e., the Kingdom of Heaven—which he declares is at hand. (Matthew 4:17; Mark 1:15).

The ubiquitous stories of healing are an essential part of the gospel picture; to speak of Jesus on God's mission is to speak of Jesus healing. Author Avery Brooke quips, "so much of Jesus' ministry was a ministry of healing that if you took a copy of the gospels and cut out all mention of healing or the casting out of demons, all you would have left would be paper lace."[53]

Students sometimes ask if I think when Jesus was healing he was giving Reiki. My answer is unequivocally "no." Even implying such a thing would be offensive to many Christians, for that suggestion makes light of Jesus' standing as the second person of the Trinity; i.e. the Son of God.

We have no way to know—nor do we need to know—specifically how Jesus healed. We know that he stood boldly at the juncture of both the divine and the human, and offered healing in breathtaking ways. I expect the full range of God's energy flowing through Jesus would most likely encompass every healing vibration known to us and well beyond!

Our own efforts at healing seem the merest echo of Jesus' power, yet such healing energy as we do have flows from the same Source. The Apostle Paul calls healing a spiritual gift, and writes that all such gifts flow from God. The Holy Spirit, he continues, helps us to "understand the gifts bestowed on us by God." (1 Corinthians: 2:12b) He elaborates in Chapter 12.

*To each is given the manifestation of the Spirit for the common good. To one is given through the Spirit the utterance of wisdom, and to another the utterance of knowledge according to the same Spirit, to another faith by the same Spirit, **to another gifts of healing by the one Spirit**, to another the working of miracles, to another prophecy, to another discernment of spirits, to another various kinds of tongues, to another the interpretation of tongues. All these are activated by one and the same Spirit, who allots to each one individually just as the Spirit chooses.* (1 Corinthians 12:7-11; boldface print added)

Paul asserts that these spiritual gifts are manifested by the Spirit "for the common good." Certainly it is true that people drawn to the healing ministry—including ministries of healing such as Reiki—express a desire to help others as a primary motivation. As recipients of God's bounty it is natural for us to want to share those gifts with others.

Apparently spiritual gifts are not as rarified as we have sometimes believed. Paul evidently felt that such gifts, healing included, were sufficiently common to warrant some general teaching on the topic, and so he writes to the early church communities offering clarification.

Paul's teachings on these gifts are found throughout his writings, and his is not a lone voice. The book of Hebrews points out that God testified to Jesus as messiah through "signs and wonders and various miracles, and by gifts of the Holy Spirit, distributed according to his will." (Hebrews 2:4)

In James' pastoral letter we are told that,

"Every generous act of giving, with every perfect gift, is from above, coming down from the Father of lights...." (James 1:17a)

We may say that it is a truth universally acknowledged that spiritual gifts flow from God. Since healing is a spiritual gift, it too—in all its manifestations, including Reiki healing—comes from God.

The Gospel of Healing

Matthew, Mark, Luke and John all refer to Jesus' ministry as one of preaching, teaching and healing. Their descriptions of Jesus journeying through Galilee followed by ever-growing crowds are poignant.

And he went about all Galilee, teaching in their synagogues and preaching the gospel of the kingdom and healing every disease and every infirmity among the people. So his fame spread throughout all Syria, and they brought him all the sick, those afflicted with various diseases and pains, demoniacs, epileptics, and paralytics, and he healed them. And great crowds followed him from Galilee and the Decapolis and Jerusalem and Judea and from beyond the Jordan. (Matthew 4:23-25; see parallel readings in Mark 1:39, Luke 6:17-19, and John 7:14-15)

Imagine masses of people hopefully following Jesus from town to town, struggling to walk or carry the sick, pressing close to touch him and be healed, straining to hear him speak. None of the gospels report that Jesus ever refused to heal anyone—including those of other faiths, such as the centurion (Matthew 8:5-14) or the Canaanite/ Syrophoenician woman. (Matthew 15:21-28, Mark 7:24-30) For more detailed commentary on Jesus' initial hesitancy with the Canaanite/Syrophoenician woman, see Chapter Six.

The gospel portrait of Jesus is that of a man wholly/holy dedicated to the welfare of God's people. He clearly believed that healing the body could lead to healing of the soul—and vice versa. After the forgiveness of sin, physical healing could follow. After tending to physical needs—feeding the hungry or mending withered or leprous limbs—minds and spirits could be made whole. Jesus offers sustenance to the entire being.

Although Jesus continually stresses the importance of things spiritual—

> "...do not be anxious about your life, what you shall eat, nor about your body, what you shall put on. For life is more than food, and the body more than clothing." (Luke 12:22b-23)

—he also urges the people to trust that God knows their physical needs and will provide for them.

> "Therefore do not worry, saying, 'What will we eat?' or 'What will we drink?' or 'What will we wear?'....indeed your heavenly Father knows that you need all these things. But strive first for the Kingdom of God, and his righteousness, and all these things will be given to you as well." (Matthew 6:31,32)

Jesus insists that God's compassion and love take precedence over the rigid laws of the Jewish religious and political hierarchy. Often he heals people on the Sabbath, flouting Jewish law and serving notice to the religious leaders that the Sabbath exists to serve the people, not the other way round. Frequently he touches and heals people considered ritually unclean, to the fury of the authorities. To do these things was to risk death, yet Jesus never faltered; such was his zeal for healing.

For Jesus, "healing and deliverance were not merely 'signs and wonders'; together with preaching, they **were** the central focus of His Kingdom message."[54] (emphasis added) Through his actions and through his words, over and over again Jesus announced that the kingdom of God was at hand.

As followers of Jesus Christ we are invited to be as committed to healing as he was. The traditional Christian healing methods of prayer, the laying on of hands and anointing can be as enriched by the addition of Reiki healing as they are by the wisdom and efficacy of Western medicine.

Christ's Healing Mission

Jesus knew that his time was limited, and so he prepared the disciples to carry on after he was gone. One aspect of their training is described in detail in Luke 9: Jesus gives his disciples power and authority to heal and sends them out on a mission to spread the good news of the kingdom.

Then Jesus called the twelve together and gave them power and authority over all demons and to cure disease, and he sent them out to proclaim the kingdom of God and to heal. He said to them, "Take nothing for your journey, no staff, nor bag, nor bread, nor money—not even an extra tunic. Whatever house you enter, stay there, and leave from there. Wherever they do not welcome you, as you are leaving that town shake the dust off your feet as a testimony against them." They departed and went through the villages, bringing the good news and curing diseases everywhere. (Luke 9:1-6; see also Matthew 10:1-23; Mark 6:7-13; and Luke 10:1-20)

When the gospels refer to the casting out of demons, many believe that this referred to some sort of physical dis-ease being cured. Still others take such references more literally. However, the point remains the same. In whatever way these remarks are understood theologically, medically or psychologically, "casting out demons" is a phrase which always connotes an important form of healing.

The description of the disciples' training for mission contains two elements that parallel Reiki training. First, the passage indicates that Jesus "gave" the twelve the power to cure disease. Although we do not know specifically how he did this, the text recalls the Reiki initiation process, in which the Reiki master formally and ritually passes (gives) the Reiki (divine energy) to the student. (See Chapter Four, the Attunements section)

This channeling of God's healing power is an accepted part of the Christian tradition; it is why we pray for others, and is evident when we invoke the Spirit's presence in the sacraments.

A situation described by Agnes Sanford offers a fascinating look at how we share divine energy with one another. Sanford found herself exhausted and frustrated after praying—and failing—to heal a child whose downward spiral of illness finally led him to the brink of death. Seeking counsel from "an older and more experienced prayer-worker from a neighboring city" she was given the following instruction:

> *She then directed me to go to the little boy at a certain time and place my hands upon him. 'But don't try to do anything, dearie,' she advised me. 'You've been trying too hard, and it's upset you. Just be still and know;* **He is God and His power is flowing into you through me**.'[55] (boldface added*)*

Revisiting our gospel story of the sending out of the twelve disciples, in Chapter Ten Luke goes on to add that later Jesus chose seventy others and sent them out also, to cure the sick and proclaim "The Kingdom of God has come near to you." The seventy return full of joy at the power they have been given, and Jesus reminds them that the power is not the point; the point is their entry into the Kingdom. "...do not rejoice at this, that the spirits submit to you, but rejoice that your names are written in heaven." (Luke 10:1-20; some ancient sources read "seventy-two.")

There is no recording of an extensive interview process before the seventy were chosen, nor of any test they had to pass to determine if they really had the gift of healing. They were willing, they were faithful and committed, they were chosen—and so they went.

The gospel account of the healing mission of the twelve and the seventy, and Paul's letter to the Corinthians, clearly imply that the ability to heal is more widespread than we recognize. This dovetails with the Reiki assertion that anyone desiring to do so can learn to use their God-given abilities to heal. As Dr. Usui wrote, "All beings into whom life has been breathed have received as a gift the spiritual ability to heal."[56]

The New Testament confirms that healing is a spiritual gift to be passed on and utilized for the good of all. Jesus' life and actions provides these writers—and us—with ample evidence that healing is a crucial part of God's mission. Thus the contemporary Church is encouraged to carry on in Jesus' healing footsteps and assist his work of healing creation and bringing in the Kingdom.

United in Christ

At the end of the ninth chapter of Luke there is a remarkable passage:

John answered, "Master, we saw someone casting out demons in your name, and we tried to stop him, because he does not follow with us." But Jesus said to him, "Do not stop him; for whoever is not against you is for you." (Luke 9: 49-50)

In making this remark, Jesus asserts that the act of healing performed by this man—in Jesus' name—aligns the healer with Christ. The disciples are jealously guarding their teacher's authority, but Jesus declares they need not do so; the man's words and actions place him in accord with Jesus' mission on behalf of God. Jesus is not interested in religious affiliation or professional qualification, only in the fact that the man is working in the Lord's name.

Jesus' tolerance illustrates his radical openness and his passion for the healing mission. The text provides powerful evidence that a Reiki practitioner working in the name of Christ would do so with the blessing of Christ.

The following text further highlights Jesus' remarkable inclusiveness. In the former case Jesus accepted the man as a worker in the vineyard although he was not an "official" disciple. In this next case Jesus recognizes his kinship not only with those offering healing, but also with those in need of healing.

"Lord, when was it that we saw you hungry or thirsty or a stranger or naked or sick or in prison, and did not take care of you?" Then he will answer them, "Truly I tell you, just as you did not do it to one of the least of these, you did not do it to me." (Matthew 25:44b-45)

Jesus claims that alleviating someone's suffering is the same as alleviating the suffering of Jesus himself. By inference, to neglect such a call is to neglect and wound Christ himself. Because Jesus is in us and we are in him, what happens to one happens to the other; a hurt in any part of the body is felt in the whole.

Understanding the vital importance Jesus placed on the healing mission encourages us to help and to heal in Jesus' name and with Jesus' passion. It provides the Christian Reiki practitioner, and all those in the healing ministry, with the inspiration and motivation to continue to work in Christ's name.

The Healing Fruits of God

Some Christians fear that Reiki healing may be "of the devil" rather than of God. The text below clarifies this misunderstanding, and should offer reassurance to anyone with this concern.

> *Then they brought to him a demoniac who was blind and mute; and he cured him, so that the one who had been mute could speak and see. All the crowds were amazed and said, "Can this be the Son of David?" But when the Pharisees heard it, they said, "It is only by Beelzebul, the ruler of the demons, that this fellow casts out the demons." He knew what they were thinking and said to them, "Every kingdom divided against itself is laid waste, and no city or house divided against itself will stand. If Satan casts out Satan, he is divided against himself; how then will his kingdom stand? If I cast out demons by Beelzebul, by whom do your own exorcists cast them out? Therefore they will be your judges. But if it is by the Spirit of God that I cast out demons, then the kingdom of God has come to you. Or how can one enter a strong man's house and plunder his property, without first tying up the strong man? Then indeed the house can be plundered. Whoever is not with me is against me, and whoever does not gather with me scatters....Either make the tree good, and its fruit good; or make the tree bad, and its fruit bad; for the tree is known by its fruit."* (Matthew 12:22-37; see also Mark 3:22-27 and Luke 11:14-23)

Jesus heals the man possessed by a demon, to the great disapproval of the Pharisees, who accuse him of using the power of Beelzebul (Satan) to do so. Jesus' response is cogency itself: Why would Satan want to heal someone of demonic possession?

Jesus emphasizes that only the power of God can overcome the power of evil, and he adds that one can tell good from evil by simply looking at the fruit produced. A devilish tree produces devilish fruits; a godly tree produces godly fruits.

Healing, including Reiki healing, bears the godly fruits of peace, gratitude and love. It is of God.

REIKI & THE GOSPELS

CHAPTER SIX

Gospel Healing and the Spirit of Reiki

This chapter presents a sampling of gospel healing stories. After each story is brief commentary highlighting pertinent features of the story from the viewpoint of Christian healing— including Reiki healing.

Although many of these stories appear more than once in the gospels, we will focus on just one version of each tale. Other variations are noted so different accounts may be easily accessed and compared.

I hope these vignettes will offer you inspiration and illumination as you consider the role of healing in the life and ministry of Jesus Christ and in your own life.

The Leper: Matthew 8:1-4

Christ in Friend and Stranger

> *When Jesus had come down from the mountain, great crowds followed him; and there was a leper who came to him and knelt before him, saying, "Lord, if you choose, you can make me clean." He stretched out his hand and touched him, saying, "I do choose. Be made clean!" Immediately his leprosy was cleansed. Then Jesus said to him, "See that you say nothing to anyone; but go, show yourself to the priest, and offer the gift that Moses commanded, as a testimony to them."*
>
> See also Mark 1:40-25 and Luke 5:12-14

Healing touch has sturdy roots in the Christian tradition. This particular tale describes Jesus choosing to touch a leper and thereby knowingly contravening the Mosaic purity code of the Jews. By touching this man, Jesus shows himself willing to become ritually unclean, and therefore "untouchable."

Ironically, after healing the leper and violating Mosaic law, Jesus then pointedly demonstrates respect for that same law. He instructs the healed man to "go show yourself to the priest, and offer the gift that Moses commanded, as a testimony...." Jesus thereby signals respect for the law unless it contravenes a higher law—God's divine law of love, which demands compassionate treatment of all. The law, Jesus insists, exists for the people, not vice versa.

Through his compassionate touch Jesus restores the leper to internal and external wholeness. No longer an outcast according to religious law, tradition and practice, the man can regain his place as an accepted member of the community.

Few of us will ever meet a leper, although we will meet many labeled unclean or undesirable. Jesus asks us to treat their suffering as if it is his suffering—as if it is our own suffering—for we are all one through the bond of the Spirit.

Jesus' expectation has stunning implications for all Christians, not least for those in the healing ministry. If we turn away in distaste from need or pain, we neglect Christ and diminish one another. Like the early Christians, who were justly famed for their compassion and care of others, we are called to do what we can.

Recently a priest friend of mine told me about a "down and out" fellow who showed up at a meeting at her well-to-do church. He was in search of a meeting himself—an AA meeting—and clearly he badly needed one. She told him he was in the wrong place and gave him directions to the correct church. After he left my friend found herself distracted for the rest of the meeting, and regretful the next day. "Christ showed up at that meeting," she told me. "And I was too busy to give him the attention he needed."

Christ shows up in our lives on a daily basis. May we have eyes to see him, hearts and minds filled with compassion and loving kindness—and God's healing touch.

Christ be with me, Christ within me,
Christ behind me, Christ before me,
Christ beside me, Christ to win me,
Christ to comfort and restore me.
Christ beneath me, Christ above me,

Christ in quiet, Christ in danger,
Christ in hearts of all that love me,
Christ in mouth of friend and stranger.

Part of the hymn traditionally called
St. Patrick's "Breastplate" Prayer

The Centurion and the Slave: Luke 7:1-10

Faith and Healing

After Jesus had finished all his sayings in the hearing of the people, he entered Capernaum. A centurion there had a slave whom he valued highly, and who was ill and close to death. When he heard about Jesus, he sent some Jewish elders to him, asking him to come and heal his slave. When they came to Jesus, they appealed to him earnestly, saying "He is worthy of having you do this for him, for he loves our people, and it is he who built our synagogue for us." And Jesus went with them, but when he was not far from the house, the centurion sent friends to say to him, "Lord, do not trouble yourself, for I am not worthy to have you come under my roof; therefore I did not presume to come to you. But only speak the word, and let my servant be healed. For I also am a man set under authority, with soldiers under me; and I say to one, 'Go,' and he goes, and to another, 'Come,' and he comes, and to my slave, 'Do this,' and the slave does it." When Jesus heard this he was amazed at him, and turning to the crowd that followed him, he said, "I tell you, not even in Israel have I found such faith." When those who had been sent returned to the house, they found the slave in good health.

See also Matthew 8:5-13

One of the notable things about this story is the lack of healing touch—in fact, the lack of physical proximity. Jesus meets neither the centurion nor his sick slave face to face, but he sends forth his intention for healing, and the slave is cured.

Jesus healing the slave from a distance recalls the offering of healing prayer for those not in our immediate vicinity. It also echoes the Reiki practice of sending healing energy to those in need of it. The Holy Spirit transcends the barriers of space and time, and Jesus utilizes the Spirit's full capabilities.

Jesus knows that he can heal the slave from a distance; what he finds astonishing is that the centurion knows it, too. For this is not simply a story about healing, it is a story about faith. The centurion, whose religion is never revealed but who is clearly not Jewish, reveals himself to be a man of deep faith. He so trusts Jesus' healing authority, and therefore God's, that he believes the healing can take place even from a distance. No wonder Jesus is amazed.

Although neither one is Jewish, Jesus responds to the centurion's request and to the slave's need. He looks beyond religious identity to the faith in the centurion's heart—a radical departure from the prevailing attitudes of the time. Sadly, it is a radical departure from some attitudes even today.

Jesus' disregard of religious boundaries recalls Reiki founder Mikao Usui's assertion that Reiki can be learned by anyone, of any (or no) religious persuasion, for it is "built upon the spiritual power of the universe" rather than upon religious tenets.[57]

The ability to heal or be healed lies beyond religious affiliation, race, gender, age, socio-economic standing or any other requirement we care to name. Healing energy is universally available, for it flows from the One Source, the God of All.

The Gerasene (Gadarene) Demoniacs: Luke 8:26-39

Healing Choices

Then they arrived at the country of the Gerasenes, which is opposite Galilee. As he stepped out on land, a man of the city who had demons met him. For a long time he had worn no clothes, and he did not live in a house but in the tombs. When he saw Jesus, he fell down before him and shouted at the top of his voice, "What have you to do with me, Jesus, Son of the Most High God? I beg you, do not torment me"—for Jesus had commanded the unclean spirit to come out of the man. (For many times it had seized him; he was kept under guard and bound with chains and shackles, but he would break the bonds and be driven by the demon into the wilds.) Jesus then asked him, "What is your name?" He said, "Legion"; for many demons had entered him. They begged him not to order them to go back into the abyss.

Now there on the hillside a large herd of swine was feeding; and the demons begged Jesus to let them enter these. So he gave them permission. Then the demons came out of the man and entered the swine, and the herd rushed down the steep bank into the lake and was drowned. When the swineherds saw what had happened, they ran off and told it in the city and in the country. Then people came out to see what had happened, and when they came to Jesus, they found the man from whom the demons had gone sitting at the feet of Jesus, clothed and in his right mind. And they were afraid. Those who had seen it told them how the one who had been possessed by demons had been healed. Then all the people of the surrounding country of the Gerasenes asked Jesus to leave them; for they were seized with great fear. So he got into the boat and returned. The man from whom the demons had gone begged that he might be with him; but Jesus sent him away, saying, "Return to your home, and declare how much God has done for you." So he went away, proclaiming throughout the city how much Jesus had done for him.

See also Matthew 8:28-34 and Mark 5:1-20

I once heard of a young revival preacher who had amazing healing powers. When he was just beginning his career and was eager to make his mark, he received word that an elderly farmer had just died, so the young preacher rushed to the man's home, ready to raise a second Lazarus. But the man's wife refused to let the young fellow in the door—apparently, the last thing she wanted was her husband returned to the land of the living!

The reaction of the townsfolk to the healing of the demoniac reminds me of that farmer's wife. Rather than responding as we might expect and being pleased for the (former) demoniac—or even grateful that the neighborhood has been released from a volatile situation—instead they ask Jesus to leave town. Had they been consulted about this healing beforehand, like the farmer's wife they apparently would have said no.

We often make assumptions about people's desire for healing, but experience doesn't always bear out such assumptions. Sometimes there are surprising reasons for someone to remain unwell. Illness may bring with it attention and sympathy, which may be hard to relinquish. Or the caregiver may enjoy feeling needed and being in charge. We cannot know what the pay-off was for the farmer's widow, but clearly she considered life without her husband a big improvement. (His opinion on the matter was unavailable.)

Perhaps the townspeople in our gospel story feel having a miracle worker around destroying herds of swine at a single blow is too steep a price to pay for the healing of a single demoniac. Certainly they are terrified at the power Jesus unleashes when exorcising the demons—power beyond their understanding and certainly beyond their control. In the end they prefer the presence of a deranged demoniac to the presence of Christ.

Our dysfunctional patterns can run deep, and we don't like it when anyone tampers with them. Change hurts, so we struggle desperately to stay in our comfort zones, clinging to old behaviors though we know they're unhealthy. Sometimes it's just easier to keep our issues chained up like that demoniac, rather than set them free and have to face them.

Jesus accedes to the townspeople's request; he departs. Similarly, God invites us into wholeness but will not interfere with our right to choose. We in the healing ministry need to follow Jesus' example, and honor the choices people make for themselves.

That's not the end of the story, though, for God never gives up on our health and wholeness. Remember the prodigal son or the lost sheep or the lost coin? Whenever we are ready, God is there.

The Paralytic & his Four Companions: Mark 2:1-12

Healing without Judging

When he returned to Capernaum after some days, it was reported that he was at home. So many gathered around that there was no longer room for them, not even in front of the door; and he was speaking the word to them. Then some people came, bringing to him a paralyzed man, carried by four of them. And when they could not bring him to Jesus because of the crowd, they removed the roof above him; and after having dug through it, they let down the mat on which the paralytic lay. When Jesus saw their faith, he said to the paralytic, "Son, your sins are forgiven." Now some of the scribes were sitting there, questioning in their hearts, "Why does this fellow speak in this way? It is blasphemy! Who can forgive sins but God alone?" At once Jesus perceived in his spirit that they were discussing these questions among themselves; and he said to them, "Why do you raise such questions in your hearts? Which is easier, to say to the paralytic, 'Your sins are forgiven,' or to say, 'Stand up and take your mat and walk'? But so that you may know that the Son of Man has authority on earth to forgive sins"—he said to the paralytic—"I say to you, stand up, take your mat and go to your home." And he stood up, and immediately took the mat and went out before all of them; so that they were all amazed and glorified God, saying, "We have never seen anything like this!"

See also Matthew 8:28-34 and Mark 5:1-20

In this story the four people carrying the paralytic are willing to do just about anything to get him to Jesus for healing. We don't know how far they had carried the fellow, but it can't have been easy. When they arrive at the house in Capernaum and cannot get near Jesus, they (incredibly) climb up on the roof and dismantle a portion of it. Finally, they lower a paralyzed and helpless man through the ceiling into a crowded room!

Remarkably, no one is recorded as expressing concern at such goings on, though it must have been not only risky but noisy too. Still, the crowd receives the invalid into their midst with evident aplomb. Only when Jesus absolves the man of his sins does the atmosphere ignite.

Jesus' absolution clearly indicates the man's sinful behavior is at the root of his dis-ease, and the paralytic accepts this. He silently receives forgiveness, and his physical healing follows. When Jesus tells him to take his mat and return home—as a sign to the muttering scribes that he, Jesus, has authority to forgive sins—the man "immediately" does so.

Although Jesus knew what had caused the paralytic's illness, we should proceed with caution before acting as if we know what is at the root of any particular dis-ease. We may think we understand fully, but such situations can be incredibly complicated. If we—intentionally or otherwise—blame someone for his or her illness, we risk adding shame, confusion, fear and anger to an already complex situation.

Reiki practitioners, Christian or otherwise, are not in the business of diagnosis. We are not physicians, and behaving as if we are creates all sorts of problems. We simply offer God's healing energy through prayer and touch to those who desire it. The Spirit knows best where and how the recipient can utilize the energy. In the end, it is comforting to remember that God is God—and we are not.

Jairus' Daughter and the Woman with the Hemorrhage: Mark 5:22-43

Open to Healing

This passage from Mark contains two intertwined healing stories: that of the woman with the hemorrhage, and the story of Jairus' daughter.

Then one of the leaders of the synagogue named Jairus came and, when he saw him (Jesus), fell at his feet and begged him repeatedly, "My little daughter is at the point of death. Come and lay your hands on her, so that she may be made well, and live." So he went with him.

And a large crowd followed him and pressed in on him. Now there was a woman who had been suffering from hemorrhages for 12 years. She had endured much under many physicians, and had spent all that she had; and she was no better, but rather grew worse. She had heard about Jesus, and came up behind him in the crowd and touched his cloak, for she said, "If I but touch his clothes, I will be made well." Immediately her hemorrhage stopped; and she felt in her body that she was healed of her disease. Immediately aware that power had gone forth from him, Jesus turned about in the crowd and said, "Who touched my clothes?" And his disciples said to him, "You see the crowd pressing in on you; how can you say, 'Who touched me?'" He looked all around to see who had done it. But the woman, knowing what had happened to her, came in fear and trembling, fell down before him, and told him the whole truth. He said to her, "Daughter, your faith has made you well; go in peace, and be healed of your disease."

While he was still speaking, some people came from the leader's house to say, "Your daughter is dead. Why trouble the teacher any further?" But overhearing what they said, "Jesus said to the leader of the synagogue, "Do not fear, only believe." He allowed no one to follow him except Peter, James, and John, the brother of James. When they came to the house of the leader of the synagogue, he saw a commotion, people weeping and wailing loudly. When he had entered, he said to them, "Why do you make a commotion and weep? The child is not dead but sleeping." And they laughed at him. Then he put them all outside, and took the child's father and mother and those who were with him, and went in where the child was. He took her by the hand and said to her, "Talitha cum," which means, "Little girl, get up!" And immediately the girl got up and began to walk about (she was 12 years of age). At this they were overcome with amazement. He strictly ordered them that no one should know this, and told them to give her something to eat.

See also Matthew 8:28-34 and Mark 5:1-20

Both of these stories involve people suffering so deeply they risk public condemnation to seek healing. In Jairus' case, knowing his child may die galvanizes him to search out the itinerant rabbi and wonder worker, Jesus, despite the fact that he, Jairus, as leader of the synagogue, holds a very establishment position. He could endanger both his social position and his livelihood by involving Jesus, who is not remotely an establishment figure. Yet so great is Jairus' desperation, he even allows Jesus access to his daughter after she has died and traditional funeral activities are under way.

The woman with the hemorrhage also risks much by approaching Jesus. Touching a male stranger is shockingly brazen for any woman of that time, but especially so for a woman ritually impure due to a blood flow. Pushing through the crowd to Jesus, brushing against people along the way, is a desperate act. No wonder she comes "in fear and trembling" and falls down before him when Jesus asks who touched him. Breaking social and religious codes places her in danger of grievous consequences. Only the highest stakes—chronic illness, social isolation, bankruptcy after paying countless doctors—could drive her to behave so boldly.

All of us have at least a nodding acquaintance with social and/or religious judgment. Certainly most Christian Reiki practitioners have been thrust into the position of explaining and defending our use of Reiki. It seems odd and sometimes quite tiresome that we must defend such an effective healing method, but so it is.

On the other hand, there are many people who are open to learning about energy medicine. As in the cases of Jairus and the hemorrhaging woman, pain often provides an impetus for folks to try something new. On a flight to California, as I waited in line for the restroom, a flight attendant confided in me that his back was "killing" him. I explained about Reiki and he asked me to work on him for a few moments, which I did in the back galley under the interested eyes of everyone in line for the bathroom. Fifteen minutes later his pain was gone and he was so thrilled he presented me with a free glass of wine. Coincidentally, I was sitting next to a cardiologist who had noticed the situation as he waited in the bathroom line. The doctor was quite intrigued, asked me a number of questions, and commented that he was going to find out more about Reiki.

When it comes to God and healing, doors open in the most surprising ways.

Healing the Blind Man: Mark 10:46b-52

The Courage to Ask

There are several tales in the gospels in which the blind are healed, although each incident has a slightly different theological thrust. Mark's story—the earliest recorded and packed with lively detail—names the blind man: Bartimaeus.

> *As he and his disciples and a large crowd were leaving Jericho, Bartimaeus son of Timaeus, a blind beggar, was sitting by the roadside. When he heard that it was Jesus of Nazareth, he began to shout out and say, "Jesus, Son of David, have mercy on me!" Many sternly ordered him to be quiet, but he cried out even more loudly, "Son of David, have mercy on me!" Jesus stood still and said, "Call him here." And they called the blind man, saying to him, "Take heart; get up, he is calling you. So throwing off his cloak, he sprang up and came to Jesus. Then Jesus said to him, "What do you want me to do for you?" The blind man said to him, "My teacher, let me see again." Jesus said to him, "Go; your faith has made you well." Immediately he regained his sight and followed him on the way.*
>
> See also Matthew 9:27-31,
> Matthew 20: 29-34, Luke 18:35-43

Blind Bartimaeus sits by the busy road into Jericho in all weathers, trapped in his own personal darkness and begging passersby for help. Unlike the paralytic, whose friends pulled the roof off a house to get him to Jesus, Bartimaeus is alone. We see plainly how alone he really is, for when word comes that Jesus of Nazareth is passing by, no one in the crowd offers to help Bartimaeus attract the attention of the famous healer. Instead they tell him to be quiet.

What courage it must take to sit, day after day, asking for help from people you can't see. As Jesus comes walking along,

Bartimaeus displays his courage yet again. He shouts out Jesus' name, over and over: "Jesus, Son of David, have mercy on me!" The crowd "sternly" orders him to stop, but Bartimaeus ignores them and calls out "even more loudly," displaying that mix of determination and desperation which has driven so many to Jesus for help, then and now.

Bartimaeus can't see Jesus' progress along the road, but he can surely hear the clamor that accompanied Jesus' public appearances. Bartimaeus raises his voice, adding to the pandemonium, when suddenly, "Jesus stood still." He stops walking, stops touching, stops greeting people—because he has heard that insistent voice. "Call him here," he instructs the crowd.

The woman with the flow of blood may have trembled at Jesus' sudden attention, but blind Bartimaeus "throws off his cloak, springs to his feet," and makes his way toward the sound of Jesus' voice.

Bartimaeus may be physically blind, but in important ways he sees clearly. Instead of remaining trapped in darkness, he does the wisest thing possible—he calls out for help. He prays. Loudly. "Jesus, son of David, have mercy on me!" He prays repeatedly, until he is heard.

Too often people say, "Others have much worse problems than I do," as if there is a scarcity of divine time and energy. The good news is, we needn't struggle to figure out what is prayer-worthy, because God is always available. To assume otherwise is to limit the nature of God. Whether we are simply going about our daily business, or whether we are laying our hands on someone in healing, we are invited to ask for God's help.

Jesus exhorts us to ask for what we need, and to repeat our requests as often as necessary. Reread the stories of the unjust judge (Luke 18:1-8) and the friend at midnight. (Luke 11:5-13) God wants to give us good things. "So I say to you, Ask, and it will be given you; search, and you will find; knock, and the door will be opened for you." (Luke 11:9) Never does he tell anyone to just put up with a problem.

Bartimaeus' prayer, "Lord Jesus Christ, have mercy on me," has been used by Christians through the centuries, often with prayer beads. It is short, works well as a repetitive mantra—which is how Bartimaeus used it—and is unspecific in terms of remedy, allowing the Spirit to work freely. We are indebted to the blind beggar from Jericho.

Christian hope never ends. We believe that God can enlighten our darkness, bring wholeness and healing from brokenness, and resurrection from crucifixion. When we call out for help the response comes, just as it did for blind Bartimaeus: "What do you want me to do for you?"

The Mute Demoniac: Matthew 12:22-29

Blinded to Christ

> *Then they brought to him a demoniac who was blind and mute; and he cured him, so that the one who had been mute could speak and see. All the crowds were amazed and said, "Can this be the Son of David?" But when the Pharisees heard it, they said, "It is only by Beelzebul, the ruler of the demons, that this fellow casts out the demons." He knew what they were thinking and said to them, "Every kingdom divided against itself is laid waste, and no city or house divided against itself will stand. If Satan casts out Satan, he is divided against himself; how then will his kingdom stand? If I cast out demons by Beelzebul, by whom do your own exorcists cast them out? Therefore they will be your judges. But if it is by the Spirit of God that I cast out demons, then the kingdom of God has come to you. Or how can one enter a strong man's house and plunder his property, without first tying up the strong man? Then indeed the house can be plundered."*
>
> See also Matthew 9:32-34 and Luke 11:14-23

The healing of the demoniac causes "all the crowds" to exclaim in amazement—all but the Pharisees, a strict sect of the Jews who respond by accusing Jesus of using the power of Beelzebul (Satan) to heal the demoniac. A debate ensues and Jesus ripostes the Pharisees' charges, declaring that Satan is not in the business of doing good works, since to do so would weaken his own kingdom. "If Satan casts out Satan, he is divided against himself; how then will his kingdom stand?"

Jesus reminds the Pharisees that their own exorcists cast out demons; do *they* use Satan's power to do so, he asks ironically? He goes on to assert that only the Spirit of God has enough strength to take on the powers of darkness—to "enter a strong man's house"—and set the prisoners free. The fact that Jesus has done so is a sign that "the kingdom of God has come to you."

Jesus' answer is helpful for anyone wondering about the use of Reiki—the energy of God—in Christian healing. When we consider the role of Reiki in healing, we will recall that:

- Jesus never withheld healing from those in need.
- Jesus asserted that the forces of evil are not in the business of healing.
- Jesus explained that the fruits of any action proclaim it to be of God or otherwise.

Compassion, healing, and peace—all benefits of Christian healing, including Reiki healing—are clearly godly fruits. Those of us who have found Reiki an effective tool in Christian healing can be confident that our efforts, offered in the name of Christ, are gratefully encouraged by Christ. If we meet a critic who feels otherwise, let us emulate Jesus and respond calmly, then move on.

Blindness can be self-inflicted. May we remain clear-sighted enough to see God's hand at work within and all around, and may we actively seek to support God's mission of healing.

The Man with the Withered Hand: Luke 6:6-11

Knowing Ourselves, Knowing God

On another Sabbath he entered the synagogue and taught, and there was a man there whose right hand was withered. The scribes and the Pharisees watched him to see whether he would cure on the Sabbath, so that they might find an accusation against him. Even though he knew what they were thinking, he said to the man who had the withered hand, "Come and stand here." He got up and stood there. Then Jesus said to them, "I ask you, is it lawful to do good or to do harm on the Sabbath, to save life or to destroy it?" After looking around at all of them, he said to him, "Stretch out your hand." He did so, and his

hand was restored. But they were filled with fury and discussed with one another what they might do to Jesus.
See also Matthew 12:9-14 and Mark 3:1-6

There are a number of gospel stories in which Jesus defies Jewish law and heals on the Sabbath. In this instance he seems to make a special point of doing so, since he calls the man with the withered hand over to him rather than waiting until the man approaches. Jesus knew precisely what the scribes and Pharisees would be waiting to see, and pointedly asks if they think it's more lawful to save life or destroy it on the Sabbath. Receiving no answer, he proceeds with the healing—the penalty for which could be death. Again he demonstrates the vital importance of healing.

Although the scribes and Pharisees are avidly watching and hoping "they might find an accusation against" Jesus, they are shockingly unconcerned about the plight of the man with the withered hand. He is simply a pawn in the political/religious game to entrap Jesus. Small wonder Mark's version of this story mentions that Jesus looks at his critics with anger, grieved at their hardness of heart. The scribes and Pharisees have twisted a well-intentioned law to justify ignoring someone's suffering. Mix this with a belief that sin causes illness and the result is a deadly recipe for callousness.

This story raises important questions for those of us in the healing ministry: when, how, to whom and why we are offering healing energy?

Like most people in our overscheduled society, we are faced with the challenge of keeping our lives in some sort of balanced state. We are what Caroline Myss labels "mystics without monasteries"; people deeply committed to seeking the inner life, yet living in the busyness of the outer world.

Facing our limitations is particularly hard for those of us in the helping professions; we want to "fix" everybody. But despite our willingness, there is only a finite supply of time and energy. Even Jesus withdrew to soak in God's presence, refreshing himself in order to continue serving effectively. If Jesus needed such regular rejuvenation, how can we do without it?

Author Richard Carlson offers some practical advice in his book *Don't Sweat the Small Stuff*. Every time someone throws us a ball, he writes, we are not bound to catch it. Refraining from being overzealous helps us avoid feeling victimized and overwhelmed. Otherwise we may be planting the seeds for exhaustion, emotional meltdown, and eventually physical illness.

Organizing our schedules and deciding where we will put our energy are choices that we make, with guidance from the Spirit. One benefit of Christian healing—including Reiki healing—is that God's energy washes through the giver as well as the recipient, leaving both feeling refreshed and invigorated. Still, even the healing ministry makes energetic demands on us, and we need to know our own limits.

Had the Pharisees and scribes in our story been self aware enough to examine their motives, they might have joined Jesus in grieving at their behavior—and hopefully done something to change it. Instead, refusing to abandon their own agenda, they use a fellow creature's misfortune as a weapon to attack Jesus.

Our own motivations to help, or not help, need regular examination. Offering—or withholding—assistance for doubtful or unclear reasons is a signal that we have some inner work to do.

The following prayer, the Collect for Purity taken from the Episcopal service of Holy Communion, offers a lovely entry point for self-examination.

Almighty God, to you all hearts are open, all desires known, and from you no secrets are hid: Cleanse the thoughts of our hearts by the inspiration of your Holy Spirit, that we may perfectly love you, and worthily magnify your holy Name; through Christ our Lord. Amen.[58]

The Canaanite (Syrophoenician) Woman: Matthew 15:21-28

The Open Heart

Jesus left that place and went away to the district of Tyre and Sidon. Just then a Canaanite woman from that region came out and started shouting, "Have mercy on me, Lord,

Son of David; my daughter is tormented by a demon." But he did not answer her at all. And his disciples came and urged him, saying, "Send her away, for she keeps shouting after us." He answered, "I was sent only to the lost sheep of the house of Israel." But she came and knelt before him, saying, "Lord help me." He answered, "It is not fair to take the children's food and throw it to the dogs." She said, "Yes, Lord, yet even the dogs eat the crumbs that fall from their masters' table." Then Jesus answered her, "Woman, great is your faith! Let it be done for you as you wish." And her daughter was healed instantly.

See also Mark 7: 24-30

There are some parallels between this story and the healing of the Roman centurion's slave. The Canaanite woman, like the centurion and his servant, is a Gentile. Just as Jesus recognizes the centurion as a man of extraordinary faith, so he comes to recognize the exceptional (and persistent!) faith of the Canaanite woman. Finally, Jesus heals the Canaanite woman's daughter from a distance, just as he healed the centurion's slave.

Love for her child leads the Canaanite woman to "the son of David," as she titles him, despite the substantial obstacles separating them: gender, religion, and ethnicity.

While the story's themes are familiar, Jesus' behavior is distinctly unusual. Generally, it's he who is on the receiving end of hostile comments, but this time he is the one who makes the provocative statement. "It is not fair to take the children's food and throw it to the dogs." Why is he initially so unhelpful and even unkind to this woman?

Some scholars point out the mitigating circumstance that Jesus, as we know from Mark's version of this story, has just withdrawn from the crowds to rest, and now his intention is abruptly frustrated by the Canaanite woman. Others speculate that perhaps Jesus felt the woman was complicit in the oppression of the Jewish peasants, who were constantly pressed to supply the Gentile cities' needs. There may be truth in both of these ideas but it still seems insufficient to explain Jesus' uncharacteristically brusque behavior.

Victor Chan's *The Wisdom of Forgiveness*, an account of the time the author spent shadowing the Dalai Lama, describes an interview by Oprah Winfrey.[59] She asks the Dalai Lama, "Would you encourage the rest of the world to meditate?" His response is eyebrow raising. "Stupid question." Winfrey is embarrassed; the witnesses are dumbstruck. It is a startlingly harsh comment from a religious leader famed for his compassion.

Apparently even spiritual icons get tired and hungry and impatient and sometimes speak without thinking. The Dalai Lama, after his initial snappishness—which perhaps surprised him as much as it did Winfrey and co.—then takes the trouble to respond to her "stupid question" with care. Similarly, Jesus softens his hard line stance as the exchange with the Canaanite woman continues.

At the beginning of the incident Jesus ignores the woman's shouting, but she persists. As she continues to call out Jesus explains himself to the disciples (who want him to send her away immediately): "I was sent only to the lost sheep of the house of Israel." Finally she approaches and kneels before him, begging: "Lord, help me."

Jesus' famous answer to this supplication is horribly offensive to modern ears. But even that repudiation doesn't stop the woman, and she comes back at him with a comment both cogent and humble: "Yes, Lord, yet even the dogs eat the crumbs that fall from their masters' table."

The way the woman verbally jousts with Jesus is remarkable and even delightful. In the end Jesus is so impressed by her faith and perseverance that he changes his position; he is convinced that her request lies within the scope of his mission. "Woman, great is your faith! Let it be done for you as you wish." Once again he registers approval for those who ask for help and keep asking until they receive it.

Jesus models for us what it means to have a truly open heart and mind. He allows all that separates him from the Canaanite woman to dissolve—a remarkable attitude as healing as the exorcism itself.

May we, also, remain open to reexamination of our habitual worldviews, for they affect our lives and our healing ministries.

The Man with the Possessed Son: Mark 9:14-29

Wrestling with "Unanswered" Prayer

When they came to the disciples, they saw a great crowd around them, and some scribes arguing with them. When the whole crowd saw him, they were immediately overcome with awe, and they ran forward to greet him. He asked them, "What are you arguing about with them?" Someone from the crowd answered him, "Teacher, I brought you my son; he has a spirit that makes him unable to speak; and whenever it seizes him, it dashes him down; and he foams and grinds his teeth and becomes rigid; and I asked your disciples to cast it out, but they could not do so." He answered them, "You faithless generation, how much longer must I be among you? How much longer must I put up with you? Bring him to me." And they brought the boy to him. When the spirit saw him, immediately it convulsed the boy, and he fell on the ground and rolled about, foaming at the mouth. Jesus asked the father, "How long has this been happening to him?" And he said, "From childhood. It has often cast him into the fire and into the water, to destroy him; but if you are able to do anything, have pity on us and help us." Jesus said to him, "If you are able!—All things can be done for the one who believes." Immediately the father of the child cried out, "I believe; help my unbelief!" When Jesus saw that a crowd came running together, he rebuked the unclean spirit, saying to it, "You spirit that keeps this boy from speaking and hearing, I command you, come out of him, and never enter him again!" After crying out and convulsing him terribly, it came out, and the boy was like a corpse, so that most of them said, "He is dead." But Jesus took him by the hand and lifted him up, and he was able to stand. When he had entered the house, his disciples asked him privately, "Why could we not cast it out?" He said to them, "This kind can come out only through prayer."

See also Matthew 17:14-21 and Luke 9:37-43

Jesus descends the mountain following his transfiguration, and his re-entry is jarring. Peter, James and John are with him, but the other disciples are surrounded by a crowd and arguing with some scribes. The disciples have apparently made fruitless, and embarrassingly public, attempts to cure the boy possessed of an "unclean spirit." In Matthew's version Jesus tells the disciples that they failed because of their little faith. In Mark's story (above) he explains that intense prayer—and some ancient sources add fasting—are required to accomplish such a challenging healing.

The disciples are fortunate to have Jesus at hand when they ask, "Why can't we fix it?" Today, we often simply don't know why some people get better and some do not. We may speculate or conjecture, but we can't know.

Sometimes in these circumstances people lose their faith or become angry with a God who appears distant, unconcerned or ineffectual against the pain and injustice of the world. Assurances that God cares feel like empty words to a person isolated and weakened by suffering. The famous "Footsteps" story is a lovely attempt to respond to that old question, "Where were you, God, when (fill in the blank) happened?"

> ## FOOTSTEPS
>
> A man who has died looks back over his life and sees it as a series of footprints in the sand along a beach. He notices God's footprints right next to his during much of his life, but at particularly trying and difficult times only one set of footprints appears. He asks God why. God responds that those were the times when he carried the man.

Jesus teaches with some frequency that we need to be willing to repeat our prayer requests multiple times. He does not explain why this is, but he makes it clear that it is not because God is reluctant to answer our prayers. Quite the opposite. Whatever the reasons, Jesus encourages us to ask and keep on asking, and to trust that our prayers are heard and answered.

Books have been written on so-called unanswered prayer. I believe that every prayer is answered, but sometimes the answer involves a period of waiting—which we dislike—and at other times we simply reject the answer as unacceptable. We can speculate endlessly about genetics and environment and the laws of the universe and personal responsibility and our own free will and God's will for us, but in the end we often just don't know.

"For my thoughts are not your thoughts, nor your ways my ways," says the Lord. "For as the heavens are higher than the earth, so are my ways higher than your ways, and my thoughts than your thoughts." (Is. 55: 8-11)

Dr. Caroline Myss teaches that the single most important thing we can do for our spiritual growth is to give up the need to know why things happen as they do. She believes—as do many people of faith—that the goodness of God will ultimately override all, and that one day we will come to understand more fully. As St. Julian of Norwich famously wrote in her *Revelations of Divine Love*, "All shall be well. All shall be well. All manner of things shall be well."

Sometimes we make the mistake of expecting that our faith— or anyone's—can offer protection from loss and pain. Jesus never made such claims. Rather, his teachings encourage us to lead lives of forgiveness and love, to trust that God wants to give us good things, to know that God rejoices with us in times of happiness and will weep with us during the inevitable times of pain.

People engaged in healing ministry need to accept this mystery of unknowing, for we will need all the solace it can offer when our most earnest prayers for healing seem to have failed. At these times only personal experience of the powerful presence and tender love of God help carry us through. Only from this place can we reach out to support those who suffer, empathizing with their discouragement and dissatisfaction and standing strong with them in that hurtful place. Sooner or later, all of us will grapple with the pain of unrelieved circumstances.

In exultant joy or in desperate sadness, God is with us. Despite our doubts and fears God meets us wherever we are spiritually— even when, like the possessed boy's father, we stumble and cry, "I believe; help my unbelief, Lord."

The Man with an Unclean Spirit: Luke 4:31-37

The Cloud of Unknowing

He went down to Capernaum, a city in Galilee, and was teaching them on the Sabbath. They were astounded at his teaching, because he spoke with authority. In the synagogue there was a man who had the spirit of an unclean demon, and he cried out with a loud voice, "Let us alone! What have you to do with us, Jesus of Nazareth? Have you come to destroy us? I know who you are, the Holy One of God." But Jesus rebuked him, saying, "Be silent, and come out of him!" When the demon had thrown him down before them, he came out of him without having done him any harm. They were all amazed and kept saying to one another, "What kind of utterance is this? For with authority and power he commands the unclean spirits, and out they come!" And a report about him began to reach every place in the region.

See also Mark 1:21-28

The story of the man with an "unclean demon" (is there such a thing as a clean demon?!) raises an interesting topic, for contemporary Christians have widely various ideas about demons, the devil and their reality—or unreality. Some ministries specialize in what is popularly called "deliverance," but there are many other Christians who believe demons, the devil and hell to be states of our own consciousness. Whatever our personal beliefs may be, it seems William Shakespeare had it right when Hamlet assured Horatio, "There are more things in heaven and earth...than are dreamt of in your philosophy."[60]

The New Interpreter's Bible contends that:

Whereas today we tend to attribute symptoms to internal causes such as chemical disorders or mental illness, first-century Jews attributed similar phenomena to external powers acting on the person. Perhaps the most honest response for an interpreter is to acknowledge how limited our understanding of spiritual and demonic forces is....In his (Jesus') presence and by his word or act, human beings were delivered from their bondage, derangement, or illness and restored to wholeness. In such stories we understand God's nature and work among us even if we do not also always understand the mystery of the spiritual or demonic forces that some human beings experience.[61]

Thankfully, most of us do indeed have clearer ideas about God's presence in the world than we have about demonic forces in the world. But even our understanding of and belief in God is under constant challenge today.

As children of the Age of Reason and the Enlightenment, we pride ourselves on clear, logical thinking and scientific explanation—which can put us in conflict with faith; i.e. belief in things unseen. When it comes to the divine, sooner or later we must let go of rational argument and take that leap, for although science illuminates many things, the existence and nature of God will not be proven through scientific means.

People of faith see God at work in our lives and in the world around us. We are willing, if hesitant, to tiptoe out from behind the assurance of scientific proof onto the shifting ground where revelation and faith carry as much weight as logic. For us, the word "mystery" is not an embarrassing term, but a necessary part of the lexicon.

In the 1991 film *Leap of Faith* Steve Martin plays con man Jonas Nightingale, a cynic masquerading as a faith healer. Nightingale runs a fairly successful operation on the Christian tent revival circuit.

Then one night a lame boy is cured during one of the healing services, and Nightingale is so terrified that he runs off, hoping to leave everything and everyone—especially the God he had thought was make believe—behind. (There is a reason he shares a name with Jonah, the prophet who ran from God and ended up trapped in the belly of a whale.) Mr. Nightingale had made the mistake of thinking that he was in charge of what happened during those services of healing.

God does not fit neatly into our little boxes, although we never tire of trying. We expect God to be simply a greater, more magnificent version of ourselves, but God is ineffable; i.e., beyond our human ability to comprehend. So when we invoke God's name, we acknowledge Mystery, with a capital "M," in our lives.

Offering healing energy in the name of Christ—whether we use Reiki or some other method—is a bold move, and one to be undertaken with humility and an acknowledgement that whatever may happen is not up to us. As C.S. Lewis points out in *The Lion, the Witch, and the Wardrobe*, "It's quite all right. He'll often drop in. Only you mustn't press him. He's wild, you know. Not like a tame lion."[62]

The Deaf Man with the Speech Impediment: Mark 7:32-37

Mindful Speech, Mindful Silence

> *They brought to him a deaf man who had an impediment in his speech; and they begged him to lay his hand on him. He took him aside in private, away from the crowd, and put his fingers into his ears, and he spat and touched his tongue. Then looking up to heaven, he sighed and said to him, "Ephphatha," that is, "Be opened." And immediately his ears were opened, his tongue was released, and he spoke plainly. Then Jesus ordered them to tell no one; but the more he ordered them, the more zealously they proclaimed it. They were astounded beyond measure, saying, "He has done everything well; he even makes the deaf to hear and the mute to speak."*

One of the most notable themes in Mark's gospel is what theologians have referred to as "the Markan messianic secret." Just when we assume that Jesus wants his name talked about for the glory of God, he gets cautious, pulls back, and enjoins people to silence. There are lots of scholarly guesses as to why he does this, including speculation that he is trying to prevent the crowds from becoming so wildly unruly on his behalf that the authorities feel forced to interfere with his mission prematurely. Whatever explanation you accept, telling folks to keep the spectacular healing of the deaf mute secret was expecting more than flesh and blood could bear, and so despite Jesus' orders the good news spreads "zealously."

It's easy to sympathize with the folks spreading the story because all of us know how hard it is to keep exciting news to ourselves. We are social creatures and, good news or bad, we want to share it with somebody.

Nevertheless, no matter how difficult it is, for people in the healing ministry confidentiality is not optional. People need to know that we will respect their privacy, and to that end we follow a few basic rules.

After someone comes to you for prayer or healing touch, and then you happen to meet them out and about someplace, don't refer to the situation beyond a neutral and courteous "How are you?" If they wish to pursue the topic, they will find a way to do so. Otherwise, let it go.

Before requesting prayer for someone, ask their permission. If that is, for whatever reason, impossible, then make any prayer requests anonymous. No last names or easy-to-recognize first names should be included.

Some churches have phone prayer "chains," some have printed prayer lists, etc. Whatever format you are working with, don't take for granted that the information to which you are privy is generally known in the congregation. Quite the opposite should be assumed.

Remember that some people are intensely private about illness. You may not agree with them, wishing you could garner more prayer support or be sure meals are delivered, but they are entitled to your respect and your cooperation.

We cannot be too meticulous when observing rules of confidentiality. Even the most purely intentioned people sometimes fall into the trap of indiscretion, as happened in the story that follows.

I was once at a church that offered healing prayer in the chapel during holy communion. Parishioners lined up with prayer requests, which they told to the first team member who became available. One Sunday a parishioner whispered a request to one of the team members, asking her to pray for his anxiety and depression issues. Unfortunately, the team member was startled into gasping aloud, "YOU have anxiety and depression?!" The parishioner requesting prayer was gratified that he had hidden his struggles so well, but the team member's comment only added to his burden, because he felt as though he'd let her down. In addition, and just as importantly, the little outburst ensured that his situation was no longer private.

This prayer worker was a sincere and compassionate person—important qualities—but so is discretion. Perhaps she had not received enough training or hopefully she would have been better prepared to handle her surprise at the gentleman's prayer request. A thorough grounding is important before anyone begins to work with the parish or the public. This should include reading on the topic of healing, communal study of scriptural texts on healing, and lots of group prayer and discussion time—including discussion of tact and privacy issues.

Beware of any situation that feels like an exception to the rules. For example, when some particularly urgent prayer request comes up it may feel okay to tell one or two trustworthy people about it. After all, we reason, the more people who know, the more people who can pray, right? No. In just that way, the folks in our gospel story decided that, despite Jesus' request, they knew better. As my nephew Danny would say, only the person making the request gets to be "the decider." And if something truly urgent does come up, you can always solicit prayers without divulging circumstances or names; God knows the names and situations, after all—we don't have to.

Thoughtful speech—or the thoughtful lack of it—requires training and commitment so that if (when) the unexpected arises, you will be better able to stay focused and act appropriately.

The Blind Man of Bethsaida: Mark 8:22-26

In God Time

They came to Bethsaida. Some people brought a blind man to him and begged him to touch him. He took the blind man by the hand and led him out of the village; and when he had put saliva on his eyes and laid his hands on him, he asked him, "Can you see anything?" And the man looked up and said, "I can see people, but they look like trees, walking." Then Jesus laid his hands on his eyes again; and he looked intently and his sight was restored, and he saw everything clearly. Then he sent him away to his home, saying, "Do not even go into the village."

We have seen Jesus heal instantly with a word, a touch, or from a distance. This story, in which he tries twice before the man is fully healed, is highly unusual. It's an excellent reminder that, even when we're doing everything right, some things just take time.

This is not a message that goes down very well in our culture. We program ourselves to move faster and faster, and we design our technology to support our fast-paced lives. Heightened productivity may result from this all this rushing, but there are other much less desirable results—such as irritability and impatience when small things "get in our way."

There is an old saying that, "if it's worth doing, it's worth doing well." We have replaced that with, "If it's worth doing, it's worth doing FAST." And let's face it, even though we may be able to bake a cake in the microwave, it will be a much better cake if we take the time to put it in the oven!

Whether you read a book about Reiki or a book about healing prayer, the authors all make the same point: the more chronic a situation is, the longer it will take to turn around. This should not be a surprise, for it is true in many areas of life. For example, the longer you don't clean your house, the more time you'll need to spend clearing it up when you finally start. The more weight you gain, the longer it will take you to lose it, etc.

Perseverance is crucial when it comes to prayer; Jesus strongly advises us against giving up too soon. So we walk through lengthy healing situations with determination and hope, trusting, believing that healing is the will of God.

Immediate and breathtaking miracles of healing can and do occur. But these are not the norm, and those engaged in the healing ministry know well that time, energy and commitment are required. In Francis MacNutt's book *The Power to Heal*, he acknowledges this.

The time element in prayer often results in sick people being improved rather than completely healed, either because we haven't spent enough time praying with them or because we don't have enough spiritual power or resources to completely vanquish the illness.[63]

MacNutt goes on to list the order of improvement he has most frequently observed in response to healing prayer.

- relief from pain
- removal of side effects from treatment
- stabilization without full healing
- return of physical function without bodily healing
- true bodily healing.[64]

In MacNutt's books he refers repeatedly to healing prayer sessions that last hours or even days. Often he prays in conjunction with his prayer team, and after an hour or two they take a break and return later that day, or perhaps the next day, and again on the next. Ultimately he and/or his team might continue to meet with and pray for the person involved for weeks or months as the healing progresses.

This sort of progression sounds familiar to most experienced healing ministers. Reiki healing can be a valuable help with this time limitation, for Reiki offers a physical focus aligned with the God-created laws of nature, which encourages energy to move more quickly and effectively through the body.

At the end of the day, we are all workers in the vineyard, and we are all on God time. Thank God.

REIKI & CHRISTIAN HEALING

CHAPTER SEVEN

Jesus' Mission of Healing

This chapter offers ideas for integrating Reiki into contemporary Christian healing ministry. We begin with a review of Jesus' healing mission, and a look at the Christian healing tradition up to the present.

As we know, all four gospels stress that Jesus traveled around the region preaching, teaching, and healing, followed by large crowds. Were he to appear today the same crowds would follow him for, in terms of human need, not much has changed in the past two thousand years.

By my unofficial count there are approximately 45 gospel stories in which Jesus provides healing. They are listed at the end of this chapter, and a number of them are discussed in Chapter Six. The list could easily be expanded if we included the feeding of the hungry, the healing/saving of the woman taken in adultery, Jesus' own resurrection, etc. Healing is a very broad term.

Jesus most often healed by laying hands on people—including those who were ritually unclean. Several times he chose to heal on the Sabbath, violating Jewish law and enraging the religious authorities. Jesus was tireless in his insistence that healing was vitally important to the fulfilling of God's mission.

On some occasions Jesus healed without touch, either from a distance—as with the centurion's slave or the Canaanite woman's daughter—or in conjunction with the forgiveness of sin. Once a person's sins were forgiven, physical healing followed.

Frequently Jesus assured the receiver that, "Your faith has healed you." He also promised, "All things can be done for the one who believes." (Mark 9:23b) Clearly a lack of faith can negatively impact the performance of signs and healings. The gospel of Matthew confirms this by reporting that in his hometown Jesus "did not do many deeds of power...because of their unbelief."

(Matthew 13:58) Although healing can happen whether or not someone believes in God (the energy exists and flows whether God gets the credit or not) a faithful and willing recipient can maximize the potential power of the healing.

Agnes Sanford suggested to nonbelievers who came to her for help that they could simply label the power they recognized in the universe as "nature" if they couldn't label it God. This worked well, although when she first tried it she was filled with trepidation. Later she would comment that she should have known God was much more broadminded than she was![65]

Jesus employed a traditional folk healing method when he utilized spit in healing the deaf man with the speech impediment and the blind man from Bethsaida. (Mark 7:32-37; Mark 8:22-26) It took two attempts before the latter healing was accomplished— apparently unique in Jesus' experience, although common for us in the contemporary healing ministry. I would discourage spitting on people to heal them, but this story remains as an encouraging reminder that healing is a process that can take time and commitment—even for Jesus.

Whether we are healing through prayer and the traditional laying on of hands, through nontraditional Reiki or through the sacraments of the church, as followers of Jesus we should accord the healing ministry the same importance and passion that he did.

Healing in the Early Church

In the post resurrection church God's healing power continued to flow and the healing ministry flourished. The book of Acts records many stories of healing, and a few are outlined below.

In Acts 3, Peter and John set the tone for the new community by healing a man who was born lame. The man then enters the temple with them, "walking and leaping and praising God" while the people are filled with "wonder and amazement." (Acts 3:1-26)

The bar is high in Acts 5, as the crowds "....carried out the sick into the streets, and laid them on cots and mats, in order that Peter's shadow might fall on some of them as he came by. A great number of people would also gather from the towns around

Jerusalem, bringing the sick and those tormented by unclean spirits, and they were all cured." (Acts 5:15-16; italics added)

In Lystra Paul heals—without touch—a man crippled from birth, with the disconcerting result that the crowd enthusiastically hails Paul and Barnabas as Zeus and Hermes. Dismayed, Paul and Barnabas repudiate such idolatry, yet even then "they scarcely restrained the crowds from offering sacrifice to them." (Acts 14:8-18)

My favorite healing story from Acts is the tale of a young fellow named Eutychus, who sits in an upper window while Paul preaches. Eventually Eutychus sinks deeply into sleep "while Paul talked still longer." Eutychus then falls three floors to the ground below and is "picked up dead." However, the redoubtable Paul runs downstairs and "bending over him took him in his arms, and said, 'Do not be alarmed, for his life is in him'….And they (took) the boy away alive and were not a little comforted." (Acts 20:9-12) This must be every preacher's nightmare; literally boring someone to death!

The Book of James paints a clear picture of the healing ministry as a vital part of the early church. When a church member falls ill the community is to "call for the elders of the church" (not necessarily the clergy) "and have them pray over them, anointing them with oil in the name of the Lord. The prayer of faith will save the sick, and the Lord will raise them up; and anyone who has committed sins will be forgiven. Therefore confess your sins to one another, and pray for one another, so that you may be healed. The prayer of the righteous is powerful and effective." (James 5:14-16)

Jesus' actions were the seeds of the Christian passion for healing, but Nigel Mumford points out that the above text from James can be considered "the biblical root of the healing ministry."[66] The passage highlights the zeal of the early church for healing, delineating a specific process for healing and outlining the communal nature of the ministry.

In the second and third centuries healing was an accepted part of the Christian Way. Justin Martyr, a Greek philosopher and convert, claimed that Christians, in the name of Jesus, healed people due to the "special gifts of spiritual power God pours out upon believers." Irenaeus, a Christian apologist, wrote about all sorts of bodily infirmity and diseases that had been cured; the exorcism of demons and even the raising of the dead. And Tertullian, a lay theologian, confirmed that God could, and sometimes did, recall the souls of human beings to their bodies.[67]

By the third and fourth centuries this healing Way had begun to erode, and Agnes Sanford theorizes that:

As the early Christians departed little by little from the high standard of Christ, the power of God faded away little by little from among them....As generation after generation passed....and the power of God dimmed out from among men more and more, they placed the responsibility for this dimming-out on Him and not on themselves. There came a time when the actual working of God's power was the exception rather than the rule, and man called it a "miracle."[68]

We can hardly prove such a theory, though by the time of Saint Augustine (354-430) there are definitely fewer reports of "miraculous" healings. Avery Brooke concurs that the practice of healing was apparently "no longer a part of a common ministry in the church, but rather was an exception to the rule."[69]

Christian Healing in the Middle Ages

Once the Roman Emperor Constantine converted to Christianity in the early fourth century, persecution of Christians was officially ended and the church received an influx of new members. Now that it was easier and safer to be Christian, some of the fervor of the early church abated and fewer healings were recorded. Exceptions were the Cappadocian Fathers—Basil the Great, Bishop of Caesarea (330-379); Basil's brother Gregory of Nyssa, Bishop of Nyssa (330-395); and Gregory of Nazianzus, Patriarch of Constantinople (329-389)—who remained deeply committed to healing. They lived in the Cappadocian region which is now Turkey.

During the fifth century the role of healing in the church continued to shift, and by the reign of Pope Gregory the Great (590-604) the Christian community regarded sickness "as a discipline from God....a complete reversal of the earlier belief that

God sent health and healing power, not illness."[70] Disease became an opportunity and obligation for reparation of sin, rather than an unnatural state that could be remedied. What had been anointing for healing was now used primarily as anointing for death. The former focus on healing as a means to fuller life on this earth turned instead to readying people at life's end for their entrance into the next world.

By the ninth and tenth centuries the ministry of healing as a support for healthy living in the here and now was largely mediated to the people either through the saints and church-controlled relics and shrines, or through monks and nuns who had been legitimated as healers by their ascetic practices. Severe restrictions on food, sleep, sex and physical comfort of any sort set these individuals apart from ordinary human beings, and imbued them with an aura of divine power. The medical/herbal expertise that many pursued only enhanced their social authority and reputation for sanctity.[71]

As the cult of saints grew ever more popular in the daily life of Christians, pilgrimages in search of healing (the latter now often synonymous with repentance) increased. Inevitably, as pilgrims flocked to the shrines and the now-flourishing cathedral cities in growing numbers, abuse of such a lively revenue-producing system crept in. "Cheap grace" became available to those who could pay: donations solicited or required for viewing of relics, masses offered for a fee, the purchase of indulgences (forgiveness of sin offered in exchange for money) and the like.

When the Reformers cast their eyes over the state of Christian healing in the fifteenth and sixteenth centuries, they were quick to condemn it, enmeshed as it was in the most questionable machinations of the Church. "...Vocal minorities of theologians and lay people challenged the validity of healing miracles promoted by, and benefiting, the Catholic Church." John Calvin (1509-1562) was one of the most influential expositors of this challenge.[72] Luther also condemned efforts to manipulate God through the saints, although later in life he softened his position on healing.

But it was too late; the damage had been done and the healing ministry seemed doomed to remain the unsavory stepchild of the traditional church. This despite the fact that biblical authority was at the heart of the Reformation, and right there in holy writ were accounts of all Jesus' and his disciples' healings.[73]

Some Christians did persist in the practice of healing and were severely criticized for it. Over the next few centuries the British and American Baptists remained steadfast in their commitment to the ministry of healing, and the Mennonites and Moravians also prayed for the sick.

The Marian shrine at Lourdes, France (1858) ushered in an age of more reliable documentation of such enterprises, breathing onto them a much-needed air of gentle respectability. The breezes of change began to blow, ever so slightly.

During the 19th century Pentecostalism picked up steam, breaking away from Methodism and becoming the fastest growing Christian church in the world. A number of both respectable and charismatic healers made their appearance in the United States and Europe: the German Lutheran pastor Johann Blumhardt; the Swiss Protestant Dorothea Trudel; and the American Episcopalian and medical doctor Charles Cullis. All three were involved in establishing houses of healing in their respective countries, and their work helped to convince "every day" Christians of the validity of healing.

Healing in the Contemporary Church

The revival of interest in healing continued through the early twentieth century, perhaps encouraged by two world wars. Christian healers such as William Branham (Pentecostal), Kathryn Kuhlman (Methodist/Baptist/evangelical), Oral Roberts (Pentecostal), and Agnes Sanford (Episcopalian), stepped forward to teach, preach and heal, yet even their spectacular results failed to completely move the healing ministry from disreputable relative to accepted family member.

In the second half of the century Father Francis MacNutt, a Harvard-educated Dominican priest, appeared on the scene, highlighting the Roman Catholic charismatic healing movement. MacNutt's books and those of others laboring in the vineyard, such as Nigel Mumford and Avery Brooke, both Episcopalians, present a portrait of the healing ministry attempting to go mainstream. Brooke's work is particularly significant, in that it focuses on building a parish healing ministry, rather than the more common alternative of having such a ministry form around a gifted and charismatic individual.

By its very nature the healing ministry can be a difficult sell. We have grown accustomed to rational scientific explanation, and the healing ministry cannot offer that. There is something undeniably flashy about it, since it functions outside our normal human experience. How do you write, without sounding crazed, that you prayed for someone and their pain vanished or their cold was cured? Or what about the person whose leg lengthened or the one whose spine straightened or the other one whose strangulated hernia disappeared? What can you say about a large and lame German shepherd planting himself in front of you, clearly asking for healing hands? And how do you explain that after healing touch and prayer the dog's limp vanished?

The Rev. Nigel Mumford, director of healing at Christ the King Spiritual Life Center in Greenwich NY, acknowledges the gap between the actual events of the healing ministry and our own ability to accept them as true and real.

> As it does for most of us, my faith wavers from time to time, and I wonder if I am kidding myself. Sometimes, the healing ministry seems so miraculous and far-fetched that I begin to doubt that what I see and experience daily is really happening....Lord, I believe. Help my unbelief.[74]

No wonder talking about this ministry is such a challenge— and working in it is such a delight.

Carrying on the healing ministry, in the name of Christ, is a responsibility we must not shirk, as the sixteenth century Spanish saint Teresa of Avila recognized.

> Christ has no body now, but yours,
> no hands, no feet on earth, but yours.
> Yours are the eyes through which Christ
> looks compassion into the world.
> Yours are the feet with which Christ walks to do good.
> Yours are the hands with which Christ blesses the world.

Misconceptions About Healing

There are two misunderstandings about healing that I believe inhibit its growth and acceptance in the mainstream Christian denominations.

1. Only a few special people can heal

A belief has developed in the Christian tradition that the spiritual gift of healing is given only to the chosen few. We have rarified the gift and turned healers into rock stars, with the consequence that the average Christian would be reluctant to appear overconfident or arrogant by indicating he/she feels he could do something so illustrious as heal.

In *Healing in the Landscape of Prayer*, Avery Brooke mentions several times that those in her parish "had a certain timidity in learning about healing. It was intriguing, yes, but also a bit frightening....We did not like to think of ourselves as 'channels for God.' It seemed presumptuous. It was more comfortable to be humble." Yet in spite of the initial trepidation "we soon found that our own hands would sometimes get as hot as radiators....We were too shy to talk about it, but we knew the Holy Spirit was with us."[75]

This knowledge is precisely why we can work in healing without arrogance: we recognize that God is at work, not we. After all, it is not true humility to refuse to do what Jesus himself modeled for us. True humility is not denying the gift; it is recognizing from Whom the gift came.

Our belief that only a special few can heal manifests itself through our hesitation to pray specifically. It is ironic that we hesitate to pray for something as straightforward as a cut finger, yet every Sunday we casually pray for world peace or the end of hunger. Healers like Agnes Sanford assure us that praying for small physical needs are the easiest "prayer-projects" of all.[76]

There is no need for us to hold back from healing—and in fact, most of us don't. We all heal instinctively. If our child gets a bump and cries, we hug her and kiss the place it hurts. When we visit a friend in the hospital we take him by the hand. If we feel pain, we put our hand on the sore spot. Healing is a natural and God-given ability and we all have it.

As long as we misguidedly promote the idea that only a few special people can heal, we prevent ordinary Christians from participating in this ministry.

2. Healing happens instantly

Because we all have heard stories about miraculous and instantaneous healings, this is what we have come to expect. Yet when reading the books written by those on the front lines of the healing movement it becomes evident that for the most part healing does not take place instantaneously. Any immediate and miraculous cures that we hear about (the latter called "spontaneous remissions" by the medical community) are the exception rather than the rule. They are not impossible—nothing is impossible with God—but as a general rule this is not the way it happens.

God's energy is always sufficient, but sometimes we fall short in our ability to channel it. Imagine trying to move a million gallons of water from the ocean to a lake—and now imagine doing it using only a measuring cup.

God's healing works through the laws of nature; we cannot expect God's laws to contradict themselves. If you don't believe this, try standing in front of a faucet and praying for the water to flow up instead of down. But if we align ourselves with the laws of creation they will work with us, not against us. This is why the shifting and healing of flesh, blood and bone is generally a process rather than a single-moment event. Prayer and healing touch can speed up the natural process by infusing more energy into it, but this usually happens in fairly predictable stages rather than immediately.

Avery Brooke observes that her parish healing group grew used to results unfolding over time rather than instantly.

> It is rare to see an immediate physical change, but again and again people come back the following week to report, "I was amazed! Last week I felt so tense and tied up in knots and it all left! I slept like a baby that night and woke up feeling refreshed." [77]

Agnes Sanford affirms that healing requires not only a commitment of steadfast faith and thanksgiving, but an ongoing flow of energy as well.

Sometimes a prayer once or twice a day is sufficient, but sometimes we need to "pray without ceasing," to keep ourselves open to the continuous inflow of God's power....It is much better to keep the power flowing by continually giving thanks for it.[78]

Francis MacNutt describes hours spent in healing prayer at weekend retreats, supported by his prayer team. Follow up sessions were sometimes held with people during the weeks and months that followed.

It's impossible to calculate exactly how many hours of soaking prayer went into this extraordinary healing. Nor how many people prayed. And there is still need for more prayer for the leg still needs more healing.[79]

My own much more modest healing experience tallies with these reports. I recall when an elderly couple in a church where I worked both had to undergo surgery each within a few months of the other. First the wife fell and broke both of her shoulders, and not long after the husband needed back surgery. During the wife's recuperation she had asked me for Reiki—she was familiar with it from a demonstration we had had at church. She loved the relief from her considerable pain that our sessions offered.

Her husband quickly left the room whenever I started to do Reiki, and I suspected that although he was tolerant, he was also uncomfortable with the idea of this new (to him) healing touch method. Consequently, after his back surgery I decided not to offer him Reiki unless he asked—which seemed unlikely. I visited him and brought him communion in the hospital, but neither of us mentioned Reiki.

Shortly after his release from hospital I visited their home and found him in distress. He had developed a painful side effect that the doctor told him sometimes occurred. He was assured that the pain would "eventually" go away, but until "eventually" arrived the poor man was miserable. He, his wife and I shared communion and prayer, and then we sat and talked. The husband kept grimacing and grabbing his lower leg and I hated to leave him like that. Finally I asked, "Would you like to try some Reiki? I could sit on the floor and lay hands on your lower leg while we chat." I well remember his reply: "I'd try anything to get rid of this pain."

Sitting on the floor and making small talk is not the optimal way to offer Reiki, but it seemed the appropriate thing to do. And after about 15 minutes, the pain was gone; I can still see his look of relief. The pain returned the next day, so I stopped by and used Reiki for a few moments again until it receded. The third day the same thing happened—except the pain left and never returned. My parishioner was only slightly more delighted than I!

God's energy does the healing, but we too contribute some of our own energy: the energy of faith, of open hearts and minds, of physical energy—and of time. Without these, no matter how great the gift, few results will be manifested.

Believing that healing happens instantly sets us up for failure, for if we pray for healing and assume success will be immediate—just like we've read about or seen on TV—and it doesn't happen that way, we give up, concluding, "I must not have the gift." (See Misconception #1: Only a Special Few Can Heal)

Integrating Reiki into Christian Healing

Every parish has its own particular form of healing ministry, although all are involved in the greater healing mission of God. Truthfully, everything that the church does can broadly be considered healing, although as I use the term here I am referring to physical or mental/emotion/spiritual healing. All healing is intended to bring us into a wholeness of relationship with God, with others, and with ourselves. Living into this wholeness is beginning to live more fully into the Kingdom of God.

Whatever the situation in your parish in terms of healing, if you are a Reiki practitioner interested in becoming involved, you will need to begin by speaking to your clergy person about it. Be sure to explain that the word "Reiki" is simply the Japanese way to refer to God's healing energy. You will want to clarify that you would perform this healing method in conjunction with Christian prayer—that it actually is a physical manifestation of healing prayer—and that it involves, but does not require, touch. Often, as you know, Reiki is used with a touch on just the head, shoulders, or hands—or by working an inch or two above the body. Or Reiki can happen while your hand rests on someone's shoulder or head, and they themselves are touching the affected area. Be sure to offer a Reiki session to your cleric, so he or she can experience it firsthand.

Clergy people are often over-extended in terms of time and commitment. If you can present some ideas for the ways in which you could be involved in healing as a Reiki practitioner, and if you are willing to take the lead to begin implementing such involvement, that may help move things along. If your parish already has a healing prayer group, that is a natural point of entry for you. If there is no such group, ask your clergy person about the possibility of getting one started. Avery Brooke's description of building a parish prayer and healing ministry offers excellent step-by-step guidance for the process; you can find the appropriate section of her book in the Endnotes listed at the back of this book.[80]

You will most likely be required to receive special training before you are allowed to pursue parish healing. In the Episcopal Church this preparation is called Safe Church training, and most denominations have something similar. This training is invaluable and will teach you how to handle yourself appropriately if you are making hospital visits or the like. In this litigious climate most likely your parish insurer will (rightly) require such education, not only for the protection of those you will be visiting, but for your own and your parish's protection as well.

There is a second sort of training you may want to pursue; if you are not yet a Reiki master teacher, consider becoming one. This certification will allow you to offer free or inexpensive Reiki classes to fellow parishioners. We all have bodies and those bodies all have particular challenges. Reiki offers a very specific, systematic way to heal, and it is easily taught. Learning Reiki helps people utilize such gifts of healing as they have been given, whether for self care or for the healing support of their friends, families and fellow parishioners—and even beyond if they feel so called.

If you are able to teach some parishioners Reiki, when you have several people trained to the Second Degree, consider working with clergy to form a Parish Visitors Group for hospital patients, nursing home residents, and shut-ins. Most parishes have a lay eucharistic ministry already functioning; it is not difficult to add Reiki to this as an option. The biggest challenge is generally to convince parishioners that it doesn't always have to be a clergyperson who visits them.

If you organize a Visitors Group, your clergy will want you to see people only in pairs—common sense adherence to Safe Church procedures. This is an effective way to minister, at any rate; the more people involved, the easier it can be to shift some of the dense energies of this world.

If your church has a time set aside for adult education, this could work well for presenting ideas to the parish for a possible healing ministry. Offer to demonstrate Reiki during an adult education session. People generally find the topic and the possibilities fascinating and you will most likely receive an enthusiastic response, including lots of questions and some requests for training. Although clergy involvement in this process is crucial, there is much in the healing ministry for which the laity can take responsibility.

If you have a parish book group, consider studying Agnes Sanford's wonderful book *The Healing Light* and/or Avery Brooke's *Healing in the Landscape of Prayer*. The first is the inspiring story of a woman who learned healing through on-the-job training; the second details the creation of a parish healing ministry and offers practical suggestions for doing the same.

Consider having a traditional healing service and inviting anyone who is interested to remain afterward to receive "chair" Reiki. Reiki practitioners—in pairs—can be on hand to offer prayer and Reiki; with two people working, ten minutes per person is usually sufficient. The Reiki can begin with traditional healing prayer, and then continue in silence. As prayer energy without the speech, Reiki eliminates the beginner's fear of not saying enough or not saying the right thing.

Some churches offer Reiki before services; some sponsor Reiki Shares or Reiki Circles, in which Reiki practitioners come together and pray, discuss their practice, and share Reiki with one another.

Going slowly and growing the ministry organically is wise. After a solid foundation is laid, then other ideas such as public healing services or attending (or perhaps eventually offering) workshops and retreats will flow naturally—and will fit well into your unique context.

We need to be circumspect and patient when introducing Reiki into a parish context. But I confess that occasionally, when I have met someone more than usually resistant, I feel very impatient indeed. The following excerpt from Barbara Crafton's "The Geranium Farm" website (geraniumfarm.org/) expresses my frustrations perfectly.

Under discussion is the story of the scribes and Pharisees who can't stop talking about Jesus healing in violation of the Sabbath; they are completely oblivious to the wonder of the healing itself. She writes:

Church! It doesn't change.

You what?!? You went in and prayed with that person in the hospital, and you aren't even an official member of the prayer team? We'll have to see about that.

You did what? You had a neat idea and got some people together to talk about it without vestry approval? Who do you think you are?

Um, a child of God? Oh, never mind. I promise not to do it again.

Of course there needs to be order in an organization. And any group needs to know what's going on among its members. But groups are famous for becoming so entranced with their internal processes that they lose sight of the mission those processes are intended to support, and it seems to me that this is really a story about that, as much as it is a story about a miracle—much more of the narrative is devoted to the poor healed man having to defend his miracle to the authorities than to the miracle itself.

If we didn't think of it, it can't be any good and it might be dangerous. If we didn't authorize it, it shouldn't happen. If it's not the usual thing, there must be something wrong with it. Where are its credentials?

But every one of our traditions was once an unusual thing. If all we can ever do are the things we already do, nothing can change. It will take a miracle.

Yes.

Share It!

Whether or not you use Reiki at your parish, a dedicated Christian practitioner will constantly find ways to share it. It may be a neighbor with a migraine or someone waiting for the ambulance to arrive, but your Reiki is always there, always ready to flow at need—like the Spirit that is its source.

Daily prayer and Reiki self care keeps us in a centered place, so that when things happen unexpectedly, or when prayer is needed quickly, you will be coming from a place of peace and focus, rather than from a place of fear and agitation. We are all intimately connected with God and if we keep that connection open and healthy, with our equipment in the best possible working order then, as Agnes Sanford explains, we can plug into God's healing current just as we plug a toaster into an electric outlet.

Reiki is an amazingly effective tool that can expand the Christian healing worker's abilities to make a difference in the world. No longer do we need to feel powerless in the face of pain and suffering. Now, with God's help, we can do something about it.

Wouldn't it be lovely if no one ever had to tell the Lord that he/she couldn't be healed because "I have no one to help me into the pool?" (John 5:7)

Let us honor Jesus' passion for healing, and carry on his legacy through this ministry that is so close to his heart.

A COLLECTION OF GOSPEL HEALING STORIES

THE GOSPEL ACCORDING TO MATTHEW

Matthew 8:1-4	The Leper
Matthew 8:5-14	The Centurion and the Servant
Matthew 8:14	Simon Peter's Mother-in-Law
Matthew 8:28-34	The Gadarene Demoniacs
Matthew 9:2-8	The Paralytic
Matthew 9:18-26	Jairus' Daughter and the Hemorrhaging Woman
Matthew 9:27-31	The Two Blind Men
Matthew 9:32-34	The Mute Demoniac
Matthew 12:9-14	The Man with the Withered Hand
Matthew 12:22-37	The Blind and Mute Demoniac
Matthew 15:21-28	The Canaanite Woman
Matthew 17:14-21	The Man with an Epileptic Son
Matthew 20: 29-34	The Two Blind Men by the Roadside

THE GOSPEL ACCORDING TO MARK

Mark 1:21-28	The Man in the Synagogue
Mark 1:29-31	Simon Peter's Mother-in-Law:
Mark:1:40-45	The Leper
Mark 2:1-12	The Paralytic
Mark 3:1-6	The Man with the Withered Hand
Mark 5:1-20	The Gerasene Demoniac
Mark 5:22-43	Jairus' Daughter and the Hemorrhaging Woman

Mark 7:24-30	The Syrophoenician Woman
Mark 7:32-37	The Deaf Man
Mark 8:22-26	The Blind Man
Mark 9:14-29	The Man Whose Son has an Unclean Spirit
Mark 10:46b-52	Blind Bartimaeus

THE GOSPEL ACCORDING TO LUKE

Luke 4:31-37	The Man in the Synagogue
Luke 4:38,39	Simon Peter's Mother-in-law
Luke 5:12-14	The Leper
Luke 5:17-26	The Paralytic
Luke 6:6-11	The Man with the Withered Hand
Luke 7:1-10	The Centurion and the Slave
Luke 7:11-17	The Widow of Nain
Luke 8:1-3	Mary Magdalene
Luke 8:26-39	The Gerasene Demoniac
Luke 8:40-56	Jairus' Daughter and the Hemorrhaging Woman
Luke 9:37-43	The Man Whose Son has an Unclean Spirit
Luke 11: 14-23	The Mute Demoniac
Luke 13:10-17	The Crippled Woman
Luke 17:11-19	The Ten Lepers
Luke 18:35-43	The Blind Beggar
Luke 22:47-51	The Slave Whose Ear is Cut Off

THE GOSPEL ACCORDING TO JOHN

John 4:46b-53	The Royal Official's Son
John 5:2-17	The Man at the Sheep Gate Pool
John 9:1-41	The Man Blind from Birth
John 11:1-45	The Raising of Lazarus

BEYOND CHRISTIANITY

CHAPTER EIGHT

REIKI AND OTHER RELIGIONS

This chapter was inspired by a conversation I had with William Lee Rand several years ago at a Reiki class in Glastonbury, England. I spoke with William about this book—which was at that point a "book project"—and that brief conversation led us to speculate about Reiki and its relationship with mainstream religions and religious practices.

Do people of faith who practice Reiki, we wondered, find their religion enriches, or is enriched by, their Reiki practice? Are there obstacles to being a religious Reiki practitioner? And since Reiki is a spiritual healing method, not a religion, can it offer common ground for people of differing faith traditions? These issues and others are explored in the pages that follow.

I am grateful to Reiki Masters Gigi Benanti and William Lee Rand for putting me in touch with some of their Reiki students and colleagues who are people of religious faith. Their sources and my own have made it possible to include in this chapter interviews with members of the five great world religions: Buddhism, Christianity, Hinduism, Islam and Judaism. To provide a context for the interview material, brief summaries of each religion are offered, followed by conversations with Reiki practitioners of that particular faith.

Every person I contacted responded to questions about Reiki and their religion with great thoughtfulness, and I thank them all for their wisdom and insight.

A Short History of Buddhism

Siddhartha Gautama, the founder of Buddhism, was born around the sixth century BCE, in what is now Nepal. His father, a Hindu, ruled a small kingdom and as a prince Siddhartha lived a privileged life. He was married and a father, but he was 29 years old before he left the protected environment of the palace and saw, for the first time, old age, illness, death and poverty. His reaction to this experience was far reaching; Siddhartha rejected his princely life, left everything behind and went in search of a solution to the problem of human suffering.

Siddhartha began his journey in the way of Indian holy men who then, as now, engaged in ascetic practices to subdue the flesh. But after several years' effort this method had failed to provide an answer to his quest. He reconsidered his course and discovered the broader, gentler path that came to be known as the Middle Way of Buddhism. He found this Way by sitting beneath a Bodhi tree and meditating until his mind became very clear. Thus he attained enlightenment and with it the understanding of how to stop the endlessly recurring cycle of suffering and rebirth. From that time Siddhartha was renamed Buddha, meaning "Awakened One."

The depth of Siddhartha's awakening was evident and many followers were drawn to him. He spent the remaining years of his life (it is believed that he lived until 80 years of age) traveling the countryside, preaching, teaching and organizing a community of monks and nuns (the Sangha).

Contemporary Buddhism includes three well-known schools: Theravada Buddhism, Mahayana Buddhism, and Tibetan Buddhism. Theravada Buddhism follows closely the traditional beliefs and practices of the founder, Shakyamuni Buddha. The Mahayana tradition stresses compassion, service and the doctrine of emptiness, a doctrine so complex that it gives rise to widely various explanations. Vajrayana Buddhism has ties to Hindu Tantric practice; through yogic discipline it seeks to help one move beyond desire and attain union with Ultimate Reality. Tibetan Buddhism, embodied in the familiar and beloved figure of the Dalai Lama, incorporates teachings from both the Mahayana and Vajrayana schools.

In Buddhism, as in most faith traditions, there is considerable diversity of belief and practice. But broadly speaking Buddhism seeks to end the cycle of human suffering and rebirth through taking refuge (coming home to a place of healing) in the Triple Jewel of the Buddha (the Awakened One), the Dharma (the

Teachings), and the Sangha (the Community). This Triple Jewel, combined with the Four Noble Truths, are essential teachings of Buddhism. The Four Noble Truths state that:

1) All worldly life involves suffering
2) The causes of suffering are attachment and desire
3) These can be overcome and ended, which is Nirvana
4) The path out of craving and attachment is the Eightfold Path:
   - Right Understanding
   - Right Thought
   - Right Speech
   - Right Action
   - Right Livelihood
   - Right Effort
   - Right Mindfulness
   - Right Concentration

Buddhism eventually spread beyond the borders of India into China, Japan, other Asian countries, and ultimately to the West. As of 2012, it is estimated that there are approximately 350 million Buddhist followers worldwide. (6% of the global population)[81]

Reiki and Buddhism: Conversations

I had the honor of corresponding with the **Rev. Hyakuten Inamoto**. Mr. Inamoto is a Pure Land Buddhist monk and a well-known Japanese Reiki teacher. He studied Reiki with Chiyoko Yamaguchi, one of Chujiro Hayashi's students. Dr. Hayashi was one of the 21 teacher students trained by Mikao Usui, and was designated as his successor by Dr. Usui himself. Mr. Inamoto's translation of Dr. Usui's memorial stone and the Meiji Emperor's waka may be found in *The Reiki Sourcebook*, by Bronwen and Frans Stiene.

Mr. Inamoto explained to me that there are many diverse healing practices in the various branches of Buddhism. However, he believes that prayer is the common denominator that unites them all.

A Buddhist can address prayers for healing to the Buddhas, to Medicine Buddha, or to one or more Bodhisattvas. (A Bodhisattva is one who has achieved enlightenment but has chosen to be reborn on earth until all other beings are freed from the circle of death and rebirthing.) Such prayers for healing might include petitions for the curing of disease, for good health and for happiness.

Mr. Inamoto believes that surrendering is essential in both Reiki and Buddhist healing, and both share the same goal—that of "Satori" or "enlightenment" through spiritual practices. Mr. Inamoto finds that the Reiki healing art is a twofold practice: one is therapeutic and another is spiritual. Reiki allows him to "heal with the use of my hands the present physical suffering or pain that I find difficult to heal by word of mouth like preaching or prayers." The physical laying-on-of-hands system utilized in Reiki brings another dimension to healing practices that often focus solely upon the verbal approach. Mr. Inamoto adds that both the Reiki method of healing and the traditional healing practices of Buddhism are complementary since "healing is beyond denominations or sects."

As I was browsing among the Reiki books one day in my local Barnes and Noble store I happily discovered the *Beginner's Guide to Reiki* by **Mr. David Vennells**. Mr. Vennells is an Englishman who is both a Buddhist and a Reiki Master, and his book contains the inspiring story of his journey to health through Reiki and his faith. I am especially grateful to him for his willingness to enter into correspondence with an unknown American woman, and for his generous encouragement of this project.

Mr. Vennells credits Reiki with leading him to Buddhism, since his discovery that Dr. Usui was a Buddhist provided powerful impetus for him to learn more about that faith. He is a follower of the New Kadampa school, a Western form of Tibetan Buddhism, and he finds that Reiki and Buddhism complement one another well and share some common characteristics.

Buddhism teaches that the "pure heart" (the Dharmakaya) is the source from which all healing and all religion flow. Mr. Vennells believes that it is from this same pure heart that Reiki also flows.

In this way he finds that Buddhism and Reiki share a common origin.

Medicine Buddha is a healing method commonly utilized in Mr. Vennells' New Kadampa tradition. It is believed that Medicine Buddha assimilates the healing power of all enlightened beings, and this gathered power then becomes available to the believer through prayer, offerings, mantras and Tantric meditation for those so gifted. It is notable that Reiki also includes mantras/symbols, chant and meditation in its healing method.

Developing a mind less attached to the world, and therefore more at peace, is one of the primary goals of Buddhism. Because Reiki energy and the practice of Reiki offer a clear pathway to such peace of mind, Mr. Vennells finds that Reiki encourages a deeper experience of Buddhism. As he notes in his book, Reiki practitioners from both religious and nonreligious backgrounds have discovered spiritual renewal through Reiki, which seems to "lead people, if they wish, to a deeper awareness of their own spirituality or potential for personal growth."[82]

A Short History of Christianity

The roots of Christianity lie in the life, death and resurrection of Jesus of Nazareth, a Jew who lived in first century Palestine. The name Jesus is a transliteration of a Hebrew name, Y'shua (Joshua), and Christ is a title meaning "the Anointed One." Western Christians believe that Jesus was both fully divine and fully human, God Incarnate (in the flesh), who came to save the human race from their sins, i.e., from their broken and wounded way of life. ("Save" can also be translated as "heal;" both come from the Greek root "diasozo.")

Within Christianity there are many divisions, referred to as "denominations." But regardless of denomination, all orthodox Christians acclaim the Lord Jesus as God's Son, and follow his teachings in the ways they judge best.

Jesus was born about two thousand years ago in Bethlehem of Judea, the son of a Jewish carpenter and his young wife—Joseph and Mary. Believers claimed his birth fulfilled an ancient Jewish prophecy foretelling the coming of the Messiah, God's Anointed

One, who would bring salvation (healing) to Israel. Jesus gathered a group of twelve disciples to live, work, and study with him, and for approximately three years they traveled the countryside together as Jesus healed, taught and preached the good news (gospel) of love and forgiveness to the people. Reports of his wisdom, compassion, and miraculous capabilities circulated widely, and enormous crowds gathered to listen and be healed.

Jesus cared deeply for his people and vehemently criticized those whom he believed were oppressing them, from their own leaders to the Roman authorities. Soon the powers that be decided Jesus must be eliminated: Rome because there was zero tolerance for civil or religious unrest, and the Jewish leaders because they feared Jesus' presence would cause trouble with Rome, disturbing an already difficult relationship. After a public ministry lasting a mere few years, Jesus was betrayed by Judas, one of the twelve disciples, into the hands of Pontius Pilate, Roman Prefect. Following a grueling interrogation and savage beating, Jesus was forced to walk outside the city limits, carrying a heavy crossbar to which he would be nailed, and from which he would hang for hours, slowly suffocating. Crucifixion was a shameful and agonizing death usually reserved for dangerous criminals, yet Jesus died with words of forgiveness on his lips.

Jesus' followers were traumatized by this turn of events, and the gospels report that the turmoil increased when, the third day after his death, his tomb was discovered empty but for an attending angel who announced Jesus had risen from the dead. During the following 40 days the resurrected Jesus appeared to his disciples and other followers, teaching and preparing them to carry on God's work. Jesus assured his followers he would not abandon them, but would send them the Holy Spirit for comfort and guidance. He instructed them to go out to all nations and share his teachings, baptizing in the name of the Trinitarian God— Father, Son, and Holy Spirit. (Matthew 28:19, 20)

Jesus' disciples suffered great persecution in the years to come—all but one were eventually executed—yet they followed his final instructions so well that Christianity today comprises over two billion followers—one third of the world's population.[83]

Reiki and Christianity: Conversations

Ms. Gigi Benanti, Reiki Master, is the proprietor of the Angelic Healing Center in Norwalk, Connecticut. She is a practicing Christian and a member of the Unity Church, a community Gigi feels blessed to have found.

Unity is a non-denominational Christian church that welcomes Reiki practitioners into the fold, both accepting their healing ministry and offering encouragement to them in the form of such practices as a Reiki Healing Circle which meets on a regular basis. A community of "huggers," the "healing touch of Reiki fits and feels right to them," Ms. Benanti explains.

Prayer and meditation practice are an essential part of the church. This emphasis, combined with her particular interest in sending Reiki healing energy to those in need of it, has led Ms. Benanti to offer an e-mail Reiki Prayer Request list to her students, and also to make appropriate prayers available on her website, angelhealreiki.com. Good results flow from this ministry of healing and prayer.

Ms. Benanti credits Reiki with being a powerful force for positive change in her life. She feels Reiki—the energy that flows from God—guided her to her church, as well as into relationships with many interesting people she would not otherwise have met. And perhaps most importantly of all, she believes that Reiki has blessed her by offering a "wealth of different ideas and strategies for healing or finding my own spiritual path."

Christians have a strong belief, as do most other religions, in the efficacy of healing prayer. In Christianity this belief is practiced through verbal or centering prayer, but also through the laying on of hands. The gospels attest to Jesus' frequent use of healing touch, and both **Barbara Bancroft**, Reiki Master and Episcopalian, and the **Rev. Judy Harris**, minister in the United Church of Christ, believe that by practicing Reiki they are also practicing healing in the tradition of the Lord Jesus Christ.

Ms. Bancroft has been a member of the healing prayer group at her church for several years. Most Sunday mornings find her in the chapel, laying hands on people and praying with them. Invocation of the healing power of the Holy Spirit is a foundational practice of such prayer groups, and "now that I have learned Reiki, there are many times that I feel the Reiki as I lay my hands on for healing prayer." For her, "the Spirit and the Reiki are one." Invoking the Reiki symbols becomes, in her spiritual understanding, simply another way of asking God to be present in both those who are offering and those who are receiving prayer.

Ms. Harris finds that Reiki provides an effective way for her to connect with the divine spark found within us all. Just as Jesus healed through the use of this divine energy, just as he taught his disciples to heal, so can we. For Ms. Harris, as for Ms. Bancroft, Reiki is prayer and Reiki is Spirit, its use being "important both to my spiritual practice and to those for whom I care as I pray."

Ms. Harris recognizes that we form our prayers from words, thoughts and images, which we modify to meet the varying needs for which we are praying. In the same way, she finds Reiki easily adaptable to differing healing situations; it offers a way to pray tangibly "hands on,"—pun intended—when it is needed most. By practicing Reiki she feels her faith is expanded, preventing its being put into a box too small to contain the greatness of God.

A Short History of Hinduism

There is no one founder of Hinduism, which translates from the Sanskrit as "The Eternal Way." Rather it is a federation of loosely connected religions and cultures that began in what is now Pakistan, perhaps as long ago as seven thousand years. At that time the Aryans invaded the Indian subcontinent and Hinduism came about as the resultant mingling of Aryan beliefs with the religious traditions already present in the area. The faith developed over time as a pragmatic synthesis of competing cultural and religious ideas and beliefs.

Some consider that Hinduism's great strength is its inclusive approach to the world and its avoidance of strict dogma. Swami Vivekananda explained: "Religion is only between you and your God, and no third person must come between you." Mahatma Gandhi expressed the essence of Hinduism when he explained that "My belief in the Hindu scriptures does not require me to accept every word and every verse as divinely inspired....I decline to be bound by any interpretation, however learned it may be, if it is repugnant to reason and common sense."

There are hundreds of ancient texts within Hinduism, but the key scriptures are the four Vedas (Rig, Sam, Yajur, and Atharva), the eighteen Puranas and the great epics of *Mahabharata* and *Ramayana*.

The Vedas, the earliest, are a collection of sacred hymns praising and worshipping the various deities such as Sacred Fire. The chanting of the Vedic mantras to different drumbeat scales while offering grains, oil, milk and honey in the Sacred Fire is a practice referred to as performing Yagnas.

The Puranas speak of the lives and achievements of the various incarnations of Indian deities such as Lord Shiva and Vishnu. They also address such matters of the faith as the creation and dissolution of the Universe, the dharmic theory, meditation and yogic techniques, and worship rituals.

The Sanskrit *Mahabharata* contains the Bhagavad Gita, a famous 700-verse Hindu scripture relating the dialogue between the great Indian warrior Arjuna and the beloved Lord Krishna, just before the beginning of an historic battle. The Bhagavad Gita is a masterful summation of all the Indian Vedic and Puranic concepts and is considered of such importance that Hindus use it in the court system for the taking of oaths.

Although there are no strict ideologies in Hinduism, all Hindus practice their religion through a variety of Yogas (spiritual disciplines) such as Bhakti (loving devotion), Karma Yoga (selfless service), Raja Yoga (meditational Yoga) and Jnana Yoga (Yoga of discrimination). The purpose of all of these is to free the soul and provide pathways to the Absolute (Brahman).

Brahman is the Universal Spirit, the Ultimate, the Sum Total of All That Ever Is, Was or Shall Be. All of the lesser Hindu deities (and there are many) are a part of the Absolute; all human beings and everything that lives have an essential spark of the Divine (Brahman) within them.

Contemporary Hinduism incorporates many schools and practices, and comprises approximately 950 million believers, or approximately 14% of the world population. Inclusion and tolerance remain a great theme of Hinduism. As the well-known Rigvedic hymn states: "Truth is One, though the sages know it variously."[84]

Reiki and Hinduism: Conversations

Ms. Anuja Bakshi teaches yoga, is a holistic health counselor and practices Reiki. As a Hindu she finds that Reiki is easily compatible with the open, inclusive faith tradition that is Hinduism. In particular the practice of Ayurveda—a Hindu holistic medicine system which is becoming well known and being utilized ever more widely throughout the world—companions well with the Reiki energy and philosophy.

Ayurveda (life knowledge) has been practiced for the past seven thousand years or more in India. The four Hindu Vedas (ancient scriptures) are the source of knowledge upon which Ayurveda is based. Together with the Yogas (spiritual disciplines) and Tantra (focused and disciplined sexuality) Ayurveda offers a pathway that guides human beings to the attainment of complete harmony within the body. Such physical harmony ultimately makes possible complete union with Brahman (Absolute Consciousness or the Divine Spirit). In Hinduism this life path is called Vedanta.

Ms. Bakshi finds that Reiki fits in perfectly with the principles of Vedanta since both are holistic, both view disease as a "disharmony of the Energies of a person" and both systems "hold central a strong belief in the capacity of the individual for self-healing through balancing these Energies."

Ms. Bakshi believes that Reiki has both strengthened and deepened the meditation and prayer disciplines that she practices as a Hindu; she also finds that these disciplines in their turn make her Reiki energy stronger and more focused. "Practicing Reiki makes me a better Hindu because it makes me a better person."

Finally, Ms. Bakshi has discovered that Reiki's "simple, direct, and amazingly powerful technique of harnessing Ki for the purpose of healing oneself and others" offers an open doorway through which she can travel on her journey to the experience of Universal Consciousness.

Ms. Veena Dass is a Hindu Reiki master living and teaching in India. She kindly shared some of her considerable knowledge of ancient Hindu healing practice and explained how her practice of Reiki is quite compatible with her religious beliefs.

There are a number of healing systems and techniques mentioned in the ancient Indian scriptures but Ms. Dass points out that it is the immense healing power of Ayurveda and yogic exercises to which the "whole world is now waking up." Ayurveda, she explains, seeks to keep the body's pitta (digestive agent), vata (pranic forces) and kapha (lymphatic fluid) in proper proportion. This balance is sought through the use of herbal medicines, proper diet, appropriate exercise and daily meditation practice.

Ms. Dass adds that there are additional healing practices in the Hindu tradition that are helpful as one travels the pathway to health. A number of these are meant to "offset the effect of evil acts done by an individual in previous lives. These accumulated evil acts are considered to be the root cause of many ailments" that seem to have no other explanation in this life. Some of the methods prescribed for cleansing from such ailments and their causes are: massaging with oils, sweating induced by medicated steam baths, putting offerings into sacred fire, chanting and fasting.

Ms. Dass agrees with Ms. Bakshi that Reiki fits easily into the Hindu healing tradition, providing a simple tool that makes the universal energy found everywhere readily accessible. She believes that her faith is deeper due to her practice of Reiki, since Reiki "brings health and universal energy to the practitioner, thereby leading him towards the power of gratitude and other positive emotions like compassion and love for suffering humanity." In this way Reiki assists her on her path to wholeness and unity with the Divine.

A Short History of Islam

Islam, like Judaism and Christianity, is a monotheistic religion that arose in the Middle East. The word "Islam" may be translated as "submission," as in "submission to God." There is no founder of Islam as such, although the Prophet Muhammad is considered the final and definitive prophet in a long line of prophets including Abraham, Moses and Jesus.

Muhammad was born in Mecca at the end of the sixth century CE and was raised by an uncle. He married and was quite prosperous by the age of 24; by age 40 he had undergone a number of mystical experiences. These experiences convinced him that he was called to proclaim the word of Allah, the supreme and single God, which he did until his death at about 62 years of age.

The primary message Muhammad brought—and which is still Islam's central message—is that there is only one God (Allah) and that worshipping anyone or anything other than Allah is sacrilege. Because we human beings constantly forget about the One (the Eternal, the Absolute) we must be continually reminded. The ritual prayer to Allah at five fixed times during the day is one way of recalling Muslims to their central awareness of God.

Initially only Muhammad's family and some of his friends accepted his call as a messenger of the One God. But eventually his following grew and he became a threat to the prevailing religious and economic life of Mecca, a city with a flourishing pilgrimage trade centered around the Ka'ba, an ancient shrine containing 360 idols.

Mecca's religious leaders tried unsuccessfully to quiet Muhammad with bribes, but he was unrelenting in his criticism of Mecca's idol worship, lack of compassion for the poor, and love of material wealth. Inevitably he became an assassination target and so fled to Medina where he continued to attract followers. Military clashes erupted between Medina and Mecca, and Muhammad emerged victorious. He captured Mecca, destroyed all idols and, in a striking display of generosity and forgiveness, offered amnesty to all but four of the men involved.

The central text of Islam is the *Qur'an*, (the Recitation) which Muslims believe Muhammad received in a 23 year revelation from

God through the Angel Gabriel. The *Qur'an* in its original Arabic is held by the faithful to be an exact and unchanged record of God's words; it is the ultimate authority. The two other important Islamic texts are the Sunnah, an assembly of traditions describing the life and works of the Prophet Muhammad, and the Sharia'ah (the Law).

There are five central tenets of Islam, to which every Muslim subscribes. First is the Kalima (the confession of faith) stating that there is no deity but Allah and that Muhammad is his messenger. Second is the observance of the Salat (ritual prayer) offered five times daily while facing Mecca. The Zakat (almsgiving) is the third, requiring at least 2.5% of all one's wealth be given to those in need. Fourth is Sawm (fasting) expected of the faithful at various times and seasons including during Ramadan, the holy ninth month of the lunar year. Last is the obligation of every physically and financially able Muslim to make the Hajj (pilgrimage) to Mecca at least once in his or her lifetime.

There are approximately one and a half billion Muslims in the world today, or about 23% of the world population.[85] The two largest sects are the Sunni (about 85%) and the Shi'a. The Sunnis represent the branch of Islam that accepts Abu Bakr as the first Muslim caliph. The Shi'a sect recognizes only teachings and guidance that come through Muhammad's family, i.e. bloodline. A third form of Islam, Sufism, is outside both the Sunni and Shi'a schools and some consider it to be an extension of Islam rather than a branch of it. The emphasis in Sufism is on mysticism and divine love; its followers seek union with God through contemplation, asceticism and cultivation of the individual's heart.

Reiki and Islam: Conversations

The **Rev. Mohammad Kambiz Fereidooni** is a Muslim, a Reiki Master and a certified holistic health counselor. As his faith instructs, he prays five times daily, and as he does so he feels a strong and satisfying connection between the energy of prayer and the energy of Reiki. He finds that the energy of prayer seems to increase the flow and strength and focus of his Reiki; and that the Reiki in turn encourages calm and ease and depth in his prayer life. Through both practices he is moved beyond the material world into a place of deep trust in God and the assurance of God's presence.

Compassion and concern for others is one of the Five Pillars of Islam, just as showing kindness to others is one of the Five Reiki Ideals. Thus Mr. Fereidooni finds himself encouraged and guided to grow in love, compassion and understanding by both his religion and his Reiki practice.

Reiki plays a central role in Mr. Fereidooni's healing practice, in conjunction with other techniques such as Ayurvedic Marma Therapy, Light and Sound Therapy, and Rain Drop Technique Aromatherapy. On a personal level he uses Reiki regularly for self healing, healing his family, and sending distant healing to the world especially in support of peace.

Islamic Sufism places particular emphasis upon mysticism, divine love, and the healing that flows from them. Sufi healing practices take various forms, and **Ms. Aida Sonac**, a Sufi Reiki practitioner, remembers experiencing a particular ritual called "Caring" when she was a child.

The Caring began with a smudging of the physical space and her body. Fanning with the hands for cleansing of her aura followed and then moved into a featherlike caressing and laying on of hands involving her palms, arms, heart and shoulders. Next her cheeks were gently cupped, this movement flowing naturally into the stroking of her brow and hair downward to the nape of her neck, and finally into an entire back massage. The "Carer" completed the ritual by quietly enfolding Ms. Sonac's feet with both hands, soothing and leaving her with a sense of calm wellbeing, and by blowing on her the Gift of the Breath.

Ms. Sonac writes that this particular version of the treatment is an adapted and abridged form of Caring intended specifically for children. She has found that "The adult format (of Caring) reminds me of Reiki;" and of course the similarities—use of calm, loving touch, attention paid to the aura, and the importance of the life-giving breath—are obvious.

As exemplified in the Caring ritual, the healing traditions of Sufism and Reiki seem to both complement and parallel one another. So easily do the two fit together that Ms. Sonac wonders if "Reiki was originally a Sufi practice without visual symbols but instead with verbal vibrations (i.e., sound healing) added to the touch."

As she practices Reiki, Ms. Sonac is "deeply mindful of the sacredness of my intention and purpose, knowing in my heart that the Beloved is near and answers the prayers of those who seek Him....Surely being aligned with the Higher Order makes for a better Reiki practitioner whatever the faith."

A Short History of Judaism

Judaism is the oldest monotheistic religion practiced in the world today, its roots beginning with the patriarch Abraham approximately 4000 years ago. Abraham (originally Abram) was the first person known to reject polytheism and to worship God as One, and it is from him that the Jewish people trace their descent. God made a covenant with Abraham, the importance of which cannot be overemphasized in the Jewish faith. In this covenant God promised that if Abraham and his people kept God's laws, their descendants would be given land and would be fruitful and multiply.

Abraham's descendants eventually moved to Egypt, where they became enslaved, but several hundred years later they were freed when God chose the prophet Moses to lead them out of slavery in Egypt (the Exodus) over Pharaoh's violent objections. The journey through the wilderness to the Promised Land (the land of Canaan) took 40 years, during which time Moses climbed Mt. Sinai and received directly from God the Ten Commandments, the basic moral and ethical teachings of Judaism. These commandments are included in the first five books of the Hebrew Bible, the Torah (Law).

After the Israelites settled into their new home they eventually felt that they needed a king to lead them. God disagreed but nevertheless allowed Saul to be anointed as the first in a long line of kings. After Saul's downfall, the great King David ruled Israel, and David's famous and wise son, Solomon, became the king who built the first Temple in Jerusalem.

After Solomon's death the kingdom split into the Northern Kingdom (Israel) and the Southern Kingdom (Judah). Israel was later conquered by Assyria and many of her people were sent into exile. Not long after, Judah was conquered by Babylon, the Temple was destroyed, and many people of the Southern Kingdom also suffered exile. Seventy years would pass before the Jews of the Diaspora (dispersion) returned to Israel under the leadership of Ezra and rebuilt a much smaller version of the Temple in Jerusalem.

Herod the Great hugely enlarged the Second Temple during his reign, and it stood for 400 years until Titus, the Roman general who would become an emperor, destroyed it. All that remains of it today is a portion of the west wall, the Wailing Wall. This sacred place is set aside for grieving and praying, the wall peppered with rolled up slips of paper tucked into its cracks, written supplications to the One God who hears and knows all.

One of the primary writings in Judaism is the Hebrew Bible. This contains the Law (Torah), the history of the Jewish people, writings such as the great hymns of Israel (Psalms), the wisdom writings (e.g. Proverbs), and the revelations of the prophets. Two other texts are also central to the Jewish faith: the *Mishna*, a codification of Jewish law, and the *Talmud*, a collection of rabbinic teachings of great practical and theoretical importance.

Contemporary Judaism is diverse, and many of the world's over 13 million hereditary Jews are not religiously affiliated.[86] Those who are generally belong to one of the four main branches: Orthodox, Conservative, Reform and Reconstructionist. These four branches, with several smaller offshoots, form a continuum of religious observance ranging from the very strict to the very liberal.

Hasidism, a form of Orthodoxy, and its more modern counterpart Jewish Renewal, a contemporary spiritual exploration utilizing music and personal experience, incline toward the mystical and have an intentional healing focus.

Reiki and Judaism, Conversations

Mr. Amir Cohen, a Jewish Reiki Master living in Israel, comments that the Jewish practice of forbidding symbols or statues can sometimes make it awkward to be a Jewish Reiki practitioner. For example, referring to the Reiki energy as "God's energy," might be felt to be a form of idolatry, and in that case to give or receive Reiki would not be allowed under Jewish law. Instead, Mr. Cohen has found it more helpful to explain the Reiki energy as "universal energy" or "energy from the Source;" in this way those who might otherwise feel hesitant can be comfortable in accepting Reiki.

Surprisingly and hopefully, Mr. Cohen reports that over the last few decades the number of Jewish Reiki practitioners in Israel has increased enormously. As a result he sees that there is a mutually beneficial sharing in progress. "There are now in Israel thousands of Reiki practitioners who give Reiki treatments to many religious people, who from their side contribute more love, compassion and tolerance" to the world. Through open heartedness and generosity of spirit, Reiki and Judaism are finding ways to coexist with mutual benefit.

Rabbi Jeffery M. Silberman, Director of Spiritual Care and Clinical Pastoral Education at Danbury Hospital, in Danbury, Connecticut, points out that the healing tradition in Judaism has historically been a fringe rather than a mainstream practice; it has had a secretive, mystical and even magical quality to it. It is good news, then, that the study of the ancient Kaballah, with its heavy focus on mysticism and healing, is rapidly gaining popularity among mainstream Jews as well as other practitioners of healing. Mr. Silberman cites the writing and publishing of the book *Everyday Miracles* as a sign that healing is taking an ever more central role in Judaism. The book, written by Polsky and Wagner, explores Hasidic stories from a psychological point of view, focusing on elements and themes of healing.

In Judaism healing prayer is the foundation of the healing ministry, and Mr. Silberman chose to study Reiki because he responded to its obvious parallels with healing prayer. Pointing out that since "modern medicine has lost the art of touch, that alone makes Reiki a powerful tool" he explains that he facilitates both

Reiki use and Reiki training in the hospital. He hopes to teach the chaplains in training with him at least Reiki First Degree, and ideally Reiki training will also become part of the nursing curriculum. Currently free Reiki sessions are available to patients through a program funded by charitable donation, and the Rabbi would like to see these free sessions extended to include staff members as well.

Mr. Silberman has concerns about what he perceives as some of the "razzle dazzle" to which the simplicity of Reiki is vulnerable—he takes issue with such practices as the use of crystals, pendulums, dousing, etc. But despite his reservations regarding those particular techniques, the Rabbi believes that Reiki is a wonderfully useful form of healing prayer, and that it provides a mindful and intentional focus for his healing practice. He has happily learned that with Reiki as a part of his ministry he absolutely can make a difference.

Can I be a Person of Faith and a Reiki Practitioner?

What, then, of our original questions? Can one be a person of faith and a Reiki practitioner? The people with whom I spoke certainly think so.

Every believer interviewed, regardless of their faith, pointed out the commonalities between prayer and Reiki. The ways in which they think about and experience prayer are similar to the ways in which they understand and experience Reiki. Both prayer and Reiki, they find, offer a direct and powerful connection with the Ultimate. This connection encourages spiritual gifts such as compassion, peace of mind, love and health; and these qualities in turn deepen prayer life and Reiki energy—and so it continues.

There is one significant difference between healing prayer and Reiki. In traditional healing prayer the emphasis is on the verbal rather than the physical, but Reiki is structured differently. The mantras/symbols may be important, but the physical application of the hands is primary. Reiki focuses prayer energy in a way that is demonstrably effective.

Conscious spiritual growth necessitates purposeful focus. Religious adherents are in the habit of attending worship services, practicing daily prayer and mindfulness, and/or observing high holy days, fasting and almsgiving. Similarly, Reiki practitioners observe the daily spiritual practice of self healing, and also of praying and chanting the Reiki Ideals every "morning and evening," following Mikao Usui's admonitions.

Reiki is a healing method, not a religion, yet Reiki and religion often utilize the same vocabulary. Words like "compassion," "love," "suffering," and "healing" surface whether discussing Reiki or religion. Yet Reiki practitioners have this advantage: they can gather, think about, discuss and practice healing—without becoming mired in religious dogma.

The largest obstacles to Reiki and religion coexisting are fear and misunderstanding. If people of faith consider the gifts Reiki offers—compassion, generosity, love and health—they might conclude that Reiki and religion are not mutually exclusive, but rather complementary and in some ways even similar.

Religion and Reiki both encourage spiritual growth and wholeness of life. Each can be complementary to the other—and both can be mutually enriching. It makes sense that Reiki, a spiritual healing method, companions so well with religion.

RESOURCES

Adherents.com. 2007.
    <http://www.adherents.com/Religions_By_Adherents.html>.

Barrett, David B., and Todd M. Johnson. *International Bulletin of Missionary Research*. January 2005.

Buddhanet.net. 2012. Buddha Dharma Education Association Inc.
    <http://www.buddhanet.net./>.

Eckel, Malcolm David. *Buddhism*. The Teaching Company. Courses #685 and #686. 2001.

Letusreason.org. Let Us Reason Ministries.
    <http://letusreason.org/>.

Religioustolerance.org. 2012. Ontario Consultants on Religious Tolerance. <http://religioustolerance.org/hinduism.htm>.

Toropov, Grandon and Luke Buckles. *The Complete Idiot's Guide to World Religions.* New York: Alpha, 2004.

Vennells, David F. *Beginner's Guide to Reiki.* New York: Barnes and Noble, 1999.

Wikipedia.org. 2012. Wikimedia Foundation.
    <http://en.wikipedia.org/wiki/Jewish_population>
    <http://en.wikipedia.org/wiki/Muslim_world>
    <http://en.wikipedia.org/wiki/Buddhism>
    <http://en.wikipedia.org/wiki/Hinduism>
    <http://en.wikipedia.org/wiki/Islam>
    <http://en.wikipedia.org/wiki/Judaism>

CHAPTER NINE

REIKI STORIES

Hearing someone give fervent thanks for the help they have received from Reiki never gets stale. To see the light in their eyes and the way their whole posture and attitude change is a tremendous gift.

I offer you the following stories in the hope that they will inspire and encourage you in your own healing ministry. The first section contains my own personal experiences; the section following consists of contributions from my Reiki students and colleagues and one story from a Reiki receiver. Had space allowed we could have shared many more such tales—events that many would call miracles happen regularly when Reiki healing is involved.

To ensure confidentiality names and circumstances have been altered as necessary.

My Stories

Ever since Joyce's husband unexpectedly walked out 18 months earlier she had been having trouble eating and sleeping, fighting depression and anxiety; every day seemed another ordeal to survive. Trying to be strong for her daughter and help care for her elderly and ailing parents constantly drained away Joyce's energy. Difficulty with a weak right kidney felt like the frosting on the cake.

Joyce had heard about Reiki but never felt inclined to try it herself—until her daughter experienced it and insisted that her mother make an appointment. After some initial hesitation Joyce did so, but even as she walked into the Reiki room she was explaining apologetically to me that she really almost never felt relaxed; she didn't want me to feel badly if nothing much happened.

Joyce later told me that at first she was preoccupied with trying not to move. Then she started to worry that I must be tired, standing and holding my hands in one place for so long. But finally she began to relax—and the next thing she knew she had awakened on the Reiki table and the session was over. Realizing how exhausted she was and with no appointment immediately following, I had decided to let her nap a while.

Joyce was amazed. Getting off the table she exclaimed, "I can't believe this! I haven't slept like that or felt this calm and relaxed in 18 months." She later told me that that night she slept for six hours straight, something she hadn't done since the breakup of her marriage. She made another appointment!

I was at St. Paul's Church one morning when Ben Brockman, the Rector, came up to me and asked if I had time to do some Reiki with a parishioner. She had a terrific migraine and he wondered if I could help.

At that point I'd never actually used Reiki for a migraine so I didn't know what to expect. But I worked on the woman's head and shoulders for several minutes, and I also used a Reiki technique called (unfortunately) Psychic Surgery.

After 15 or 20 minutes she got to her feet, marveling because she felt so well; the migraine was completely gone. She was able to carry on with the project that had brought her to church originally, and she was so delighted that later that afternoon she brought me a gorgeous bouquet of hydrangeas from her back yard.

This was the day I first learned how effective Reiki and Psychic Surgery are when dealing with a painful migraine. I have used these combined techniques many times since, almost always with excellent results.

During one of my Reiki Two classes, a student shared with the group that her cousin was very ill and dying, but was terrified of death and was desperately fighting against it. His fear and agitation greatly increased his family's distress.

When we formed our class Reiki prayer circle we imagined the student's cousin in the center of the circle and we sent Reiki to him for a few minutes.

The next day my student called me to say that her cousin had calmed down that previous evening, not too long after we sent the Reiki. Several hours later he passed on peacefully. The student definitely believed that Reiki had offered peace and acceptance to her cousin. Reiki is a wonderful resource for end-of-life situations.

A friend of my son Chris was helping me in the garden. She was working as a gardener that summer and had come into contact with poison ivy while on the job. She had had a strong reaction to it and the rash was all over her face.

As we stood chatting I casually put my hand over the side of her face nearest to me, without touching the skin. Unusually for me, I didn't even ask her permission; we were just talking and I didn't give it much thought.

The next time I saw her she confessed that she had always thought Reiki sounded weird but she was rethinking that now—because the rash on the side of her face that I had Reiki'd cleared up much faster than the rash on the other side of her face!

I have an acquaintance who has very fair, pale skin. She is sensitive to the sun and things like bug bites are quite a problem. One evening when we were sitting outside a mosquito bit her and the spot immediately flared up, promising to be a 'really itchy one' as she said. When she mentioned it I put my hand over the area for a few moments and let the Reiki flow. The next time I saw her she said the spot had disappeared shortly after receiving Reiki.

When a friend of mine had surgery she was having lots of trouble sleeping while in the hospital. I visited her and she was tossing and turning, fretting and uncomfortable. She said she would try some Reiki, and almost immediately afterward she fell deeply asleep. Later she told me, 'If I had known how good Reiki was I would have asked you to do it before this.'

Kimmy had a huge amount of pain after her recent shoulder surgery. Unfortunately she is allergic to pain meds so no relief was to be found in that way. When I first saw her she said her pain level was usually an 8 out of 10.

At the end of our session together she was thrilled that her shoulder wasn't throbbing any more and her pain level had dropped by half. "I'm a believer," she declared.

During our most recent session, Kimmy noticed her arm and shoulder both twitching oddly, and burning hot. At the end of the session she was able to life her arm, pain free, twice as high as she had been able to earlier.

A while back I was assisting at a church in upstate Connecticut, and while there I trained a number of parishioners in Reiki. During this same time period the recently widowed mother of one of the church members developed very advanced lung cancer. There is never much hope after such a diagnosis and her family was devastated.

I met with the woman and we spent some time in prayer and conversation. I also offered her some Reiki, which made her start to cough. She was pleased, commenting that previously she hadn't been able to cough and clear her lungs at all.

Two of the parishioners who had learned Reiki, Marge and Barbara, then made arrangements with the woman to visit her every week. She sat in a reclining chair and listened to soothing music, while the two women gave her Reiki for 40 minutes or so.

This continued for a number of months—at which point it was determined the cancer was gone.

Several years later, she is considered cured.

From Nancy, Friend and Client

I sought out Alice after years of having no contact with her and showed up at the communion rail one Sunday while she was in the middle of the service. From there we met again and I began to tell her how my personal life had fallen apart and the medical problems that complicated my path toward healing from the trauma of betrayals and what felt like the sudden cataclysmic destruction of my future. Buddhism touts groundlessness and considers it an opportunity to learn how to be in life differently. While that is a worthy perspective and something to perhaps strive for, for most of us, and certainly me, it feels terrifying and sad to lose so much.

And so I accepted Alice's kind offer to try Reiki even though I was skeptical and even wary of energy healing, a closed mindedness that surprises me. But I'm stumbling into this. I can't seem to get the time straight, showed up on the wrong week for an appointment, even though I am a clinical psychologist with a confusing calendar I manage without a problem. I often talk throughout the sessions and when I'm not talking I'm crying, pouring my heart out into the space shared by Alice and some loving presence. What I feel is warmth from Alice's hands and at times I can feel the warmth of her fingers in a part of my body that she is not touching. I feel the safety of this person and this place and so sometimes painful feelings emerge and linger. While I'm not sure how this will unfold, I am certain that the most pronounced "mood" of the room is love and what flows is love. The way I look at it, being in the presence of love can't hurt me and may help me to find my own heart and the ability to love again.

From Geri, Reiki Master

One evening the daughter of a very dear friend of mine called to say that her mother's situation had deteriorated (the mother had been ill for some time), that she was in a coma, and if I wanted to see her alive I should come to the hospital immediately. I went to the hospice area of the hospital because my friend was expected to die at any moment. The family was eating pizza in another room when I arrived, so I had a chance to be alone with her. I entered the room and put my hand up to start the Reiki flow, and in about 20 seconds she opened her eyes, looked straight at me, and said, "Hi, Geri!" The family was overjoyed and astonished, and so was I. My friend had been in a coma for 12 hours, but after she came out of it she had three more precious weeks with her family and friends before she passed on.

From Gigi, Reiki Master Teacher

Reiki has been a great blessing in my life. It's helped me create a life that allows me to do what I have felt from childhood to be my life's mission: to help others help themselves.

When I was younger, I did some type of healing for others from my own energy, which did help people, but I would feel drained afterward. Eventually, through a teacher of meditation and healing, I was led to Reiki.

When my godson was born three months early, he had a number of medical issues and complications and was not expected to survive. I went several times to the neo-natal center with the family's permission. The first time I went, after I had done Reiki for a little while the nurses came over to me to check my hands and said, 'Whatever you were doing for this baby, please continue to do it because all the monitors are positively affected.'

The baby's mother was also in critical condition and not expected to live. The doctors had had trouble stopping her bleeding following the birth and she had needed two complete blood transfusions. She had been one of my first Reiki master students. This was well before the time when hospitals were familiar with Reiki practitioners, so the husband told the nurses I was just coming to pray with laying on of hands, which of course they were used to. And the same thing happened with the mother as had happened with the baby; the machines reacted positively and by the end of the visit the mother had moved a bit and opened her eyes. Again the nurses came in and checked my hands, and said they had wanted to see that I had nothing in my hands because the machines were so powerfully affected by whatever I was doing. And they asked me to continue. At the husband's request I returned to the hospital later that day for another Reiki visit and by then the mother had been removed from the ICU and was rapidly improving.

Both the baby and his mother survived; the baby is healthy, happy and thriving. His mother is the vice president of a large company.

I had another interesting Reiki experience several years ago when I attended a conference. We all sat down to a meal, and immediately I felt drawn to use my Reiki hands to go over the food. My hands actually hurt as I moved them over the plate and as I said "Ouch!" and pulled away I heard, "Do not touch this food or eat it. It will make you deathly ill." Well, it was the only food available that night but I didn't eat it. I went hungry but I listened. The other people at the table asked what I was doing and when I told them they asked if I would check their meals, too. I did that and then I shared with them that there were three other plates of food that shouldn't be eaten. Two were a definite "no", one was a maybe. The two people who had those meals thought this was just too weird, it looked fine and so they ate it. They ended up in the hospital with botulism. The third "maybe" person ate some of the food, started to feel uncomfortable and stopped. She had a mild case of food poisoning but saw a doctor and was better fairly quickly.

Reiki has greatly increased my self confidence. I used to be shy and aloof—not the sort of person who tells people to leave their dinners on the table uneaten! Reiki has helped prevent my getting colds and if I do get one it is milder. The few times I have hurt myself or twisted something, as active people sometimes do, by quickly giving myself Reiki I have been able to prevent any larger issue from developing.

There are many stories I could tell about Reiki, but really when I think of my own Reiki story, I mostly think of all the students I have given Reiki to since 1996. An important part of fulfilling my life's purpose of healing and helping others has been teaching Reiki to my students and knowing that they will go out and share Reiki with others, too.

From Stephanie, Reiki Master

One day I did a Reiki session for my cousin who is a reasonably open yet somewhat skeptical former academic. She had informed me that her knees were bothering her, particularly her left one. My hands have often been hot when doing Reiki, but this was unbelievable; they were on fire when I was in contact with her knees. She felt the heat as well—and her knees felt great all day and into the evening.

From Susan, Reiki Level One Practitioner

My younger son had had surgery and he was in a great deal of pain in the recovery room. The nurse had given him morphine but he was not getting much relief and was calling out for me. The nurse came and got me to try to help calm him down. She had another shot of morphine ready but was reluctant to use it with his heart condition. When I came in I started to do Reiki. It not only calmed him down but it helped with his pain. He did not need the other shot and was able to leave the recovery room shortly after. It was such a wonderful thing—and the nurse was so impressed she said she'd like to try it for her back pain.

From Denise, Reiki Master

My father was very ill and in a great deal of pain. I was at a Reiki class one day and at my request we all sent my dad Reiki, hoping it would help with his pain.

I spoke with him shortly afterward and he was remarking that his pain had left him quite suddenly. After talking to him further, I realized that his pain had gone at just about exactly the time we were sending him Reiki.

From Sandy, Reiki Master

Shortly after taking Reiki Level Two, I received a call from a friend who had been admitted to the hospital several days earlier. The friend's situation was rapidly becoming life threatening, and so of course I went to the hospital to visit her and to pray for healing. Rather than enter into intimidating and confusing explanations about Reiki, I simply said to her, 'I'm going to help you relax and through the laying on of hands you will be connected with the healing power of the Holy Spirit.' Then I laid my hands on her abdomen, and invited her to place her own hands on top of mine. We remained in that position while I prayed silently; the experience was very peaceful and calming. Afterward, we talked and laughed together—and by the next day my friend had been sent home. I believe that, in her eagerness to be healed, my friend—a very Spirit-filled person—cooperated totally and completely, and so the healing was facilitated.

One day I was at a picnic and there was a woman there who was trying to unzip her jacket but the zipper was stuck fast. Several people were gathered around trying to help, with no success. The woman was becoming quite hot and starting to get panicky, at which point I suggested, 'Let's try some Reiki.' I held my hands over the woman's heart chakra to bring some calm and relaxation into the situation. Then I put my hands over the spot where the zipper was stuck. And, as you have guessed, the zipper slid right down, to the relief of all concerned!

While I was training for the Master Level of Reiki, early one morning the barking of my two dogs drew me outside to see what was going on. When I looked over the fence I was horrified to see our neighbor's sweet but very frail 18-year-old cat "Kitty," who can hardly walk, being attacked by a Doberman pincher. The cat was pushed up against the stone wall and streaks of blood were showing on his white chest where the dog was grabbing and tearing at him.

Using a rock, a leaf rake and a lot of yelling I finally managed to drive the very determined Doberman away. Kitty's owner was unable to catch the cat, who had crawled into an inaccessible corner. Shortly afterward the owner's daughter came out to try again—but Kitty was gone. I was so sad, knowing he had probably crawled away to die.

I was still feeling badly when I left for my final Reiki Master class that afternoon. During the class five of us Reiki students gathered around a table to offer healing prayer/Reiki for those we knew who were in trouble or suffering. I shared the upsetting story about Kitty and asked that we focus our intention on him and send him divine healing energy.

The next day I received a phone message from the neighbor's daughter saying that, incredibly, the cat was back, apparently unhurt. I couldn't believe her—after all, I had seen him attacked and faltering and wounded and bloody—so I ran outside to see for myself. And sure enough, there was Kitty, sitting in the driveway across the street, so clean and fluffy he was almost radiant. There wasn't a mark on him!

From Kim, Reiki Master

I had heard about Reiki but didn't know what it was until I experienced it firsthand. My yoga teacher had become a Reiki practitioner and she did Reiki as part of our relaxation at the end of class. The energy I felt from her each time was amazing and I knew this was something I wanted to pursue, so she put me in touch with Alice and I have been her student for all three levels of Reiki.

I primarily wanted to study Reiki in order to help my mom, who suffers from a chronic disease. She has felt the benefits of Reiki. I have also been able to use Reiki on a friend and colleague at work. There was a woman in my office who was going to undergo back surgery for herniated discs. After only two short sessions of Reiki her blood pressure dropped 20 points; Reiki was able to calm and relax her.

I was at a party when a friend mentioned having a headache, and although I felt unsure about whether or not to say anything, I offered to do Reiki. The friend was so delighted at the results that she then introduced me to a young man who was having neck troubles. He was an athlete and was willing to try Reiki to ease the stiffness in his neck—and he was amazed at the results.

I believe God has guided me on this journey and that Reiki is a gift from God.

Blessings on Your Journey

I hope these stories illustrate for you some of the amazing things that can happen with Reiki healing. Whenever people share their Reiki experiences, remarkable stories are always forthcoming.

Please consider whether learning Reiki might make it possible for you to enrich your own ministry of healing.

BIBLIOGRAPHY of SOURCES

Christian Healing

Brooke, Avery. *Healing in the Landscape of Prayer.* Cambridge, MA: Cowley, 1996.

Kelsey, Morton. *Healing & Christianity*. Minneapolis: Augsburg Fortress, 1995.

Kuhlman, Kathryn. *I Believe in Miracles.* Alachua, FL: Bridge-Logos, 1962.

MacNutt, Francis. *Healing*. Notre Dame, IN: Ave Maria, 1974.
---. *The Healing Reawakening*. Grand Rapids, MI: Chosen, 2005.
---. *The Power to Heal.* Notre Dame, IN: Ave Maria, 1977.

Mumford, Nigel. *Hand to Hand.* New York: Church, 2000.

Porterfield, Amanda. *Healing in the History of Christianity*. Oxford: Oxford UP, 2005.

Sanford, Agnes. *The Healing Light*. New York: Random, 1947.

Healing

Anodea, Judith. *The Truth about Chakras.* St. Paul:Llewellyn, 1994.

Reiki

Doi, Hiroshi. *Modern Reiki Method for Healing*. Vancouver: Fraser, 2000.

Gray, John Harvey and Lourdes. *Hand to Hand: the Longest-Practicing Reiki Master Tells His Story.* Bloomington, IN: Xlibris, 2002.

Horan, Laxmi Paula. *Exploring Reiki: 108 Questions and Answers.* Franklin Lakes, NJ: New Page, 2005.

Hosak, Mark and Walter Lubeck. *The Big Book of Reiki Symbols.*
Twin Lakes, WI: Lotus, 2006.

King, Dave. O-Sensei. *A View of Mikao Usui*. 2006.
<http://www.lulu.com>.

Klatt, Oliver. *Reiki Systems of the World*. Twin Lakes, WI:
Lotus, 2006.

Lubeck, Walter, Frank Arjava Petter and William Lee Rand. *The
Spirit of Reiki*. Twin Lakes, WI: Lotus Press, 2001.

Miles, Pamela. *Reiki: A Comprehensive Guide.* New York:
Penguin, 2006.

Paul, Nina L. *Reiki for Dummies*. Hoboken: Wiley, 2006.

Petter, Frank Arjava*. The Original Reiki Handbook of Dr. Mikao
Usui.* Twin Lakes, WI: Lotus, 2002.
---. *Reiki Fire*. Twin Lakes, WI: Lotus, 1997.
---. *Reiki: The Legacy of Dr. Usui*. Twin Lakes, WI: Lotus, 2005.

Rand, William Lee. *Reiki: The Healing Touch, First and Second
Degree Manual.* Southfield, MI: Vision, 1991.

Steine, Bronwen and Frans*. A-Z of Reiki Pocketbook*. Ropley, UK: O
Books, 2006.
---. *The Reiki Sourcebook.* Arlesford, UK: O Books, 2003.

Vennells, David F. *Beginner's Guide to Reiki*. New York: Barnes and
Noble, 1999.

Reiki and Science

Moyers, Bill. *Healing and the Mind.* New York: Doubleday, 1993.

Oschman, James L. *Energy Medicine: The Scientific Basis.*
Edinburgh: Churchill, 2000.

Pert, Candace B. *Molecules of Emotion.* New York: Scribner, 1997.

Religion

Deanesly, Margaret. *A History of the Medieval Church 590-1500.*
Cambridge: Cambridge UP, 1990.

Chadwick, Owen. *The Reformation.* London: Penguin, 1964.

ENDNOTES

CHAPTER TWO

[1] Petter, Frank Arjava, *Reiki Fire*, Lotus Light Publications, Twin Lakes WI, 1997, p. 20.

[2] Ibid, p. 21.

[3] *The Holy Bible,* New Revised Standard Version, NY, NY, Oxford University Press, 1989, NT, p. 55.

[4] Stiene, Bronwen and Frans, *A-Z of Reiki Pocketbook*, O Books, Winchester UK, 2006, p. 132.

[5] Petter, Frank Arjava, *Reiki Fire, (ISBN: 9780914955504)* © Lotus Light Publications, Twin Lakes WI, 1997, pp 28-31.

[6] Petter, Frank Arjava, *The Original Reiki Handbook of Dr. Mikao Usui*, Lotus Press, Twin Lakes WI, 2002, pp. 28-65.

[7] Stiene, Bronwen and Frans, *A-Z of Reiki Pocktbook*, O Books, Winchester UK, 2006, pp. 175, 176.

[8] Petter, Frank Arjava, *Reiki—The Legacy of Dr. Usui, (ISBN:978 091495 5566)* ©Lotus Light Publications, Twin Lakes WI, 1998, p. 13.

[9] Stiene, Bronwen and Frans, *A-Z of Reiki Pocktbook*, O Books, Winchester UK, 2006, pp. 79-82.

[10] Rand, William Lee, *Reiki, The Healing Touch, First and Second Degree Manual*, Vision Publications, Southfield MI, 1998, pp. I-16 – I-17.

[11] Gray, John Harvey and Lourdes, *Hand to Hand: the Longest Practicing Reiki Master Tells His Story*, Xlibris Corportion, 2002, p. 93.

[12] Stiene, Bronwen and Frans, *A-Z of Reiki Pocketbook*, O Books, Winchester UK, 2006, pp. 38, 229, 230.

[13] Petter, Frank Arjava, *Reiki The Legacy of Dr. Usui,* Lotus Light Publications, Twin Lakes, WI, 2005, p. 13.

CHAPTER THREE

[14] Gray, John Harvey and Lourdes, *Hand to Hand: the Longest Practicing Reiki Master Tells His Story,* Xlibris Corporation, 2002, p. 76-77.

[15] "Empowering Women," a 4-CD set, Hay House Inc., 1997.

[16] www.ynhh.org/smilow...hospital/.../complementary_services.aspx, 2011.

[17] www.harthosp.org, 2011.

[18] www.mskcc.org, 2011.

[19] www.centerforreikiresearch.org, 2011.

[20] Miles, Pamela, *Reiki: A Comprehensive Guide*, Penguin Group, NY, NY; 2006, Foreword, pp 2-3.

[21] Gray, John Harvey and Lourdes, *Hand to Hand: the Longest Practicing Reiki Master Tells His Story*, Xlibris Corporation, 2002, p. 15.

[22] http://energymedicineuniversity.org/faculty/oschman.html

[23] Oschman, James L.; *Energy Medicine, the Scientific Basis*; Churchill Livingstone; Edinburgh, London, NY, NY, Oxford 2000; p 250.

[24] Ibid, pp. 5 – 7.

[25] Ibid, p. 8.

[26] Ibid, p. 178.

[27] Ibid., p. 250. (Boldface print mine)

[28] Pert, Candace B., *Molecules of Emotion*, Scribner, NY, NY, 1997, p. 18.

[29] http://en.wikipedia.org/wiki/Candace_Pert

[30] Ibid.

[31] www.candacepert.com/

[32] Pert, Candace B., *Molecules of Emotion*, Scriber, NY, NY 1997, p. 20.

[33] Moyers, Bill D., *Healing and the Mind*, Doubleday, NY, NY, p. 186.

[34] Pert, Candace B., *Molecules of Emotion*, Scribner, NY, NY, 1997, p. 245.

[35] United States Conference of Catholic Bishops; Committee on Doctrine; Guidelines for Evaluating Reiki as an Alternative Therapy, March, 2009.

[36] D. M. Eisenberg et al., "Unconventional Medicine," pp. 246-252.

[37] Miles, Pamela, *Reiki: A Comprehensive Guide*; Jeremy P. Tarcher/Penguin, NY, NY; 2006, p. 184.

CHAPTER FOUR

[38] Petter, Arjava Frank, *The Original Reiki Handbook of Dr. Mikao Usui*, Lotus Press, Twin Lakes, WI, p, 8.

[39] King, Dave, *O Sensei: A View of Mikao Usui*, Copyright Dave King 2006, p. 31.

[40] Petter, Frank Arjava, *The Original Reiki Handbook of Dr. Mikao Usui*, Lotus Light Publications, Twin Lakes WI, 2002, pp. 28-65.

[41] www.reiki.nu/history/hayashi/hayashi.html

[42] Rand, William Lee, *Reiki: The Healing Touch; First and Second Degree Manual,* Vision Publications, Southfield MI, 1991, p. 1-16.

[43] Ibid, pp. D7-D16.

[44] Gray, John Haravey and Lourdes, *Hand to Hand: The Longest Practicing Reiki Master Tells His Story*, Xlibris Corporation, 2002, p. 13.

[45] Sanford, Agnes, *The Healing Light*, Random House Publishing, NY NY, 1947, p. 20. (Italics added)

[46] Vennells, David, P., *Beginner's Guide to Reiki*, Barnes and Noble, Inc., 1999, p. xvii.

[47] Gray, John Harvey and Lourdes, *Hand to Hand: The Longest Practicing Reiki Master Tells His Story*, Xlibris Corporation, 2002, p. 79.

[48] Sanford, Agnes, *The Healing Light*, Random House Publishing, NY NY, 1947, pp. 3-4.

[49] Lubeck, Walter, *The Big Book of Reiki Symbols,* Lotus-Press, Twin Lakes, WI, 2006.

[50] Petter, Frank Arjava, Reiki website, www.reikidharma.com/

[51] Sanford, Agnes, *The Healing Light*, The Random House Publishing Group, 1947, p. 1. (italics added)

[52] Vennells, David, *Beginner's Guide to Reiki*, Barnes and Noble Books, USA, 1999, p. 81.

CHAPTER FIVE

[53] Brooke, Avery, *Healing in the Landscape of Prayer*, Cowley
    Publications, Boston MA, 02111, p. 17.
[54] MacNutt, Francis, *The Healing Reawakening*, Chosen Books, Grand
    Rapids MI, 2005, Chapter 5, "How Did Jesus See His Mission?"
[55] Sanford, Agnes, *The Healing Light*, Random House Publishing
    Group, 1947, pp. 11-13. (boldface emphasis added)
[56] Petter, Frank Arjava, *Reiki: The Legacy of Dr. Usui*, Lotus Press, Twin
    Lakes WI, 1998, p. 19.

CHAPTER SIX

[57] Petter, Frank Arjava, *Reiki: The Legacy of Dr. Usui*, Lotus Press, Twin
    Lakes WI, 1998, p. 13.
[58] *The Book of Common Prayer*, The Church Hymnal Corporation, NY,
    NY, 1979, p. 355.
[59] His Holiness the Dalai Lama, and Chan, Victor, *The Wisdom of
    Forgiveness: Intimate Conversations and Journeys,* Riverhead
    Books, NY, NY, 2004, pp. 137-138.
[60] Shakespeare, William, *Hamlet*, Act I, Scene V, Lines 159-160.
[61] *The New Interpreter's Bible*, Abingdon Press, Nashville, 1995.
    Volume IX, pp. 113-114.
[62] Lewis, C.S., *The Lion, the Witch and the Wardrobe*, HarperCollins
    Publishers, NY, NY, 1950, p. 182.
[63] Macnutt, Francis, *The Power to Heal*, Ave Maria Press, Notre Dame
    IN, 1977, pp. 57.
[64] Ibid, pp. 57-62.

CHAPTER SEVEN

[65] Sanford, Agnes, *The Healing Light*, Random House Publishing Group, NY NY, 1947, p. 56.

[66] Mumford, Nigel, *Hand to Hand,* Church Publishing, NY NY, 2000, p. 122.

[67] Kelsey, Morton T., *Healing and Christianity: A Classic Study*, Augsburg Fortress, Minneapolis, 1995, p. 119-120.

[68] Sanford, Agnes, *The Healing Light*, Random House Publishing Group, NY NY, 1947, p. 42.

[69] Brooke, Avery, *Healing in the Landscape of Prayer,* Cowley Publications, Boston MA, 1996, p. 23.

[70] Ibid, p. 24.

[71] Porterfield, Amanda, *Healing in the History of Christianity*, Oxford University Press, Oxford, 2005, p. 80.

[72] Ibid, p. 95.

[73] Brooke, Avery, *Healing in the Landscape of Prayer*, Cowley Publications, Boston MA, 1996, p. 27.

[74] Mumford, Nigel, *Hand to Hand*, Church Publishing, NY NY, 2000, p. 81.

[75] Brooke, Avery, *Healing in the Landscape of Prayer*, Cowley Publications, Boston MA, 1996, pp. 4-5.

[76] Sanford, Agnes, *The Healing Light*, Random House Publishing Group, NY NY, 1947, p. 9.

[77] Brooke, Avery, *Healing in the Landscape of Prayer*, Cowley Publications, Boston MA, 1996, p. 81.

[78] Sanford, Agnes, *The Healing Light*, Random House Publishing Group, NY NY, 1947, p. 14.

[79] MacNutt, Francis, *The Power to Heal*, Ave Maria Press, Notre Dame, IN, 1977, p. 54.

[80] Brooke, Avery, *Healing in the Landscape of Prayer,* Cowley Publications, Boston MA, 1996, pp. 51-70.

CHAPTER EIGHT

[81] buddhanet.net

[82] Vennells, David F., *Beginner's Guide to Reiki,* Llewellyn Worldwide, Ltd., 1999, p. 4.

[83] http://www.adherents.com/Religions_By_Adherents.html

[84] http://www.religioustolerance.org/hinduism.htm

[85] http://en.wikipedia.org/wiki/List_of_countries_by_Muslim_population

[86] http://en.wikipedia.org/wiki/Jewish_population

ABOUT THE AUTHOR

The Rev. Alice Mindrum is an Episcopal priest in the Diocese of Connecticut, a Reiki master teacher, speaker and writer. She has worked in the church for over two decades and finds that knowledge of Reiki enhances her ability to effectively offer pastoral care. Her previous writings include magazine articles, curriculum for the Church, and a calendar entitled "Medjugorje and the Word."

Alice lives in Fairfield County, Connecticut with her husband Tom. They have three grown sons, Jim, Chris, and Eric. Alice loves gardening, cooking, reading, writing and traveling. For more information, visit her website amhealing.com.

Made in the USA
Lexington, KY
06 April 2013